TRAVEL WITH YOUR PET

BY

Paula Weideger

AND

Geraldine Thorsten

ILLUSTRATED BY ERNIE PINTOFF

A FIRESIDE BOOK
Published by Simon and Schuster

A Fireside Book
Published by Simon and Schuster
Rockefeller Center, 630 Fifth Avenue
New York, New York 10020
First paperback printing 1974
SBN 671-21449-7 Casebound
SBN 671-21756-9 Paperback
Library of Congress Catalog Card Number: 72-83936
Designed by Irving Perkins
Manufactured in the United States of America

1   2   3   4   5   6   7   8   9   10

*To Twiggy, Lorenzo
and Louie* . . .

ACKNOWLEDGMENTS

We would like to thank the personnel at the many consulates, tourist offices, ship lines and airlines who helped us gather information. We would like to thank particularly the people in the airline cargo departments for their patience and encouragement, and the A.K.C. and the A.S.P.C.A. for providing most helpful information.

Our special thanks to Arlene Donovan and Nancy Hardin for acting as our guardian angels; to Ann Thorsten for assistance above and beyond the call of friendship and/or duty; to Francis Santamaria for proofreading on the very day of Joshua's birthday; to Mr. Albrecht of the Amstelrust Hotel in Amsterdam for being such a kind and helpful gentleman; and to Michael Labowitz, Rosalie Labowitz and Virginia Siegel for their special help and encouragement.

CONTENTS

FOREIGN AFFAIRS

INTRODUCTION

Never mind that dogs are *man's* best friend. Between the two of us we have three dogs. Louie (Paula's dog) is black and white and very shaggy and alleged to be a standard poodle. Geraldine's dogs are Twiggy and Lorenzo, chocolate-brown poodles, smaller but shaggy too. We like 'em.

I like Louie, Geraldine likes the Twig and Lorenzo. They're pets, affectionate and companionable. That is why we share our lives with them. They are hardly guard dogs.

Dogs are a part of our lives. When either of us plans a trip, we naturally think of taking our pets along. It's fun. The pleasure of traveling with a shaggy dog or two is the reason we do it. (We can rationalize that pleasure by thinking about how we will avoid the guilt that dogs left behind are so good at provoking. Then too, kennels are generally very expensive and rarely terrific places. We could go on rationalizing—no need.)

Besides the pleasure we get from traveling with our pet companions and the pleasures we like to assume they find in traveling with us, there are all sorts of bonuses found in sharing our journey with the well-traveled pet.

Touring with your pet is a certain way to avoid the experience of just "seeing" places. While seeing parts of our own country or a foreign land is often a rich experience, there are always times when you want to share and exchange your experience with other people. There are times, too, when you realize that it is difficult to make contact with local people and so you are missing a large part of the rewards your trip has to offer.

Pets are a source of an almost universal language of understanding and affection. They provide a straightforward area of mutual interest and concern. This makes meeting new people an easy matter, and since communication is based on shared caring, pets provide a far more graceful beginning than having to talk about the problems of your home city or even your country's foreign policy when you hardly know the other person.

If you are going to be traveling with children, you may have felt some concern about whether they will be lonely or bored. While walking the dog or carrying the cat, just imagine how easy it will be for your children to meet other children. They will be immediately engaged in talking about their pet and will readily lose their self-consciousness about being an outsider. In places where there are no other children around, they will still have the companionship of their pet. (This last sentence is as true for grown-up children too.)

Should your travels take you abroad you will find that tourism and tourists have become a matter-of-fact experience (and not always a pleasant one) to the people of many countries. Yet even in Paris, which has earned the reputation of being one of the places where tourists receive the coolest reception, I found that walking with Louie made me an almost instant member of the neighborhood community. It is as though you immediately lose the anonymity of being "just another tourist" and take your rightful place as another human being.

All this has been about why you should take your pet with you. Why your pet would want to go is another topic, of course. Most pets prefer the company of the people they are used to. In other words, they like going along a whole lot more than they like staying behind.

WHY THIS BOOK?

Okay. . . . Traveling with your pet can be fun and can reap countless rewards. We're writing this book to give you the kind of information needed to experience that pleasure. If you've ever spent days on the phone trying to find out what papers you need to take your cat on a trip through South America or your dog on a camping trip across country you know that the pleasures along the way start to pale as you almost sink under the weight of information-gathering.

Many people don't even start this procedure and leave their pets behind because they have been told things that just aren't true. There are, for instance, literally thousands of hotels and motels across the United States that accept pets and yet many pet owners are unaware of this. Others travel abroad without the beasts because they've heard that there's a quarantine when they come back. Not so.

We hope that the information in this book enables all of you to travel with your pets and enjoy it. If you have any experiences along the way while traveling with your pets—experiences of places especially hospitable or hostile—please do let us know.

YOUR PET AS TRAVELER

TRAINING YOUR DOG
OR CAT TO TRAVEL

_____

Naturally enough, since you love your pet you're concerned about its comfort and welfare. Traveling can and should be a safe, pleasant experience for your animal. In this chapter we will concentrate on travel from your pet's point of view and show you how easy it is to transform your dog or cat from a homebody into a happy nomad.

PRE-TRAVEL EXPERIENCES

The first thing you want to do is protect your pet from illness and prevent it from transmitting disease to other animals or to people.

Have your puppy inoculated against distemper, canine infectious hepatitis and leptospirosis when it's about 5 weeks old and again when it's 3 to 4 months old. It should have a booster shot of this multiple vaccine every year.

Your puppy should also be vaccinated against rabies when it's between 3½ to 6 months old. The time interval between inoculations will vary from 1 to 3 years, depending on the type of rabies vaccine given.

If you have a cat, be sure it too is inoculated against both rabies and distemper.

TRAINING FOR TRAVELING

Thus fortified, your pet is ready to become a traveler. If you own or have access to a car, you are indeed fortunate. You can introduce your pet to traveling as part of its general training when it's quite young. Twiggy, a medium-sized chocolate-brown poodle, was 3 months old when I (Geraldine) bought her in Rome. I commuted to work by car every day and took her with me, Italy being the tolerant country that it is. The first few trips were admittedly a bit messy, but that was due to my ignorance; they took 45 minutes, which is too long for a beginner. And once I fed her before we left, which is a mistake. But within a week she'd become a veteran traveler. She now takes to any mode of transportation with the greatest aplomb and, in fact, is so enthusiastic I have to watch to see that she doesn't jump into strangers' cars.

The whole secret to avoiding motion sickness is to start your dog or cat out on frequent short trips. Take your pet for a 10-minute ride every day for a few days. Then increase the ride to 20 minutes for the next few days, and then to 30-minute trips. Naturally, you can vary this if you want to— take your pet out every few days, or for 15-, then 30-, then 45-minute intervals. But the point is to let your animal gradually adjust its sense of balance to being in a moving vehicle.

Cats, by the way, can become superbly nonchalant travelers. As you have doubtless observed, they have an enviable ability to make themselves at home anywhere. When traveling by car, we suggest you don't keep your cat in a carrier but allow it to find its own comfortable spot, as long as it doesn't interfere with your driving.

Don't start a training session with your animal right after it has eaten. Disaster will inevitably result. Wait until a couple of hours have passed since your pet's last meal.

Also, take along your pet's favorite toy or blanket. Like our-

Your pet has feelings too.

selves, animals adapt more easily to the new, however wonderful, if they have a few old familiar objects with them.

From the very first practice trip, encourage your pet to sit or lie quietly. This problem will probably not arise with cats, but dogs can be very exuberant. And no matter how dearly you love your dog, a dog that tramples over everyone, scrambling from window to window, is a nuisance to other passengers, a dangerous distraction to the driver and, certainly, a danger to itself.

If you have children, you'd do well to include them in these practice sessions. Children are more likely to understand that the car is no place to roughhouse with their dog if they've helped with the training.

It is possible that your dog may suffer from motion sickness (drooling and/or vomiting) while it's learning. Just in case, protect the car seat and floor with plastic or some other invulnerable material, and take along some paper toweling and disposal bags.

Perhaps yours is an older dog and, either because you haven't done much traveling or were intimidated by your dog's first bouts of motion sickness, you despair of its ever being comfortable. Don't give up . . . this is one trick even an older dog can learn. My other dog, Lorenzo, was well over a year old before he gained his travel legs. Unlike Twiggy, he was raised in the harsher climes of New York City, with considerably fewer opportunities to travel. And, although quite as handsome as his mother, he's a smaller, more excitable dog. He drooled so heavily on our infrequent trips that I feared he was destined by temperament to be a stay-at-home. But a recent jaunt to Europe found us traveling by planes and trains, taxis and trams, and amidst this wealth of experience, Lorenzo swiftly adjusted. Again the key to success was frequent trips of reasonably short duration.

Incidentally, we don't recommend tranquilizers or sedatives as a means of helping your pet become a traveler.

They're necessary for plane trips, but not as an ordinary practice. Dogs and cats are very adaptable animals. If you give them medication, you are actually delaying their adjustment.

TRAVELING BY CAR

The happy day has arrived at last. Your pet has been calm and comfortable on its last, longest practice trips and now it's ready for some *real* traveling. You all climb into the car and are off for a weekend in the country. What can you do to insure that your pet is as comfortable as the rest of the family?

Just as you did for the training period: The animal should have no food within 3 hours or more of the trip, and no water an hour or so in advance. Take along its blanket and some toys. My (Geraldine's) sister's dog, Daisy, wouldn't dream of traveling anywhere without *her* favorite—a little hard-rubber valise, certainly an appropriate choice. If you're doing the selecting for your dog, we suggest a ball to play with and at least one hard, unshreddable chew toy.

If you are especially safety-conscious, you can construct a safety belt for your dog out of its harness and two leashes or pieces of rope. The dog will be most comfortable, yet safely restrained, if you attach the leashes to the sides of the harness farthest from its neck. Secure the free ends of the leashes to stable portions of the car on either side of the animal. Or secure one leash only and have someone hold the other.

The car should always be sufficiently ventilated. Fresh air is a great preventive of motion sickness and it's one of your pet's pleasures in traveling to savor new, exotic scents. Don't, however, let your dog hang its head out the window— that's too much of a good thing. It can all too easily get sharp grit in its eyes or nose, or an inflammation in its ears or throat from the wind.

Whenever you leave your pet in a parked car, be sure each window is open a few inches so that it gets enough air but is not able to climb out. During hot weather, try to park in the shade *and* open the windows. A car interior can become phenomenally, killingly hot; well over 110°F., in fact. One Australian lady returned on a scorching summer's day to find her pet canary flat on its back on the floor of its cage. As a frantic last resort, she rushed home and popped it into her refrigerator. Fifteen minutes later she found it dazed but revived, trying gamely to chirp. Since, however, this ingenious technique is neither always possible nor guaranteed of success, it seems better to take more conventional precautions.

Stop every two hours or so and let your pet out for a drink of water and some exercise. For any trip of more than an hour's duration, take along a thermos of water—keep it refilled—and a drinking bowl. Also, take along your pet's leash. Neither cats nor dogs should be allowed to dart off exploring on their own in unfamiliar territory.

TRAVELING IN A CASE

You'll usually have to keep your pet in a carrier in buses, trams and subways, plane cabins, and perhaps when boarding and leaving trains. Select a carrier that is sturdy yet lightweight and allows your pet some visibility. It should be spacious enough to permit your animal sufficient room to turn around in—unless your pet is a greyhound.

The greyhound is an extremely hyperactive animal and would pace itself frantic in a large cage. Also, its legs are very fragile and there is a real danger it might injure itself. To insure a safe, tranquil trip, confine a greyhound to the smallest carrier it can fit into comfortably. For the safety of any pet, the carrier you choose should be smoothly constructed so that your animal can't hurt itself.

Whenever possible, buy the carrier several days in advance of your trip so your pet can get used to it and make it its own. Put some of the animal's favorite toys and bedding inside and it will probably start using the carrier for its naps.

There are just a few common-sense rules to keep in mind when your pet travels in a carrier. First and foremost, place the carrier in as stable a position as possible—under your seat, on the seat next to you, or on your lap.

One of the pleasures of traveling with your pet is that an animal invariably draws people to you. Almost everyone is at least curious, and usually interested in animals. This doesn't mean though that your pet is fair game to be annoyed or teased, especially if it's in a carrier. You can discourage people in a friendly way from tapping on the case or poking at the animal. They can just as easily express their interest by looking at or talking to your pet or, better yet, to you.

In some countries—Holland and Canada, for instance—you can take your dog on the bus or tram in all its natural splendor, *sans* case, provided the dog is leashed. This is a great convenience for you but your dog may not be immediately enthusiastic about it. When Paula was living in Amsterdam, her dog, Louie, eyed Dutch trams with great initial skepticism. At first Paula was perfectly happy to go exploring on foot with Louie but that *does* get wearisome, and besides, it rains a lot in Holland. And so the fateful moment arrived when they would either be drenched or Louie would learn to like the trams. There they were at the tram stop and there was the tram. Louie, a standard-sized poodle, may be a ball of fluff but you just don't go scooping him up in your arms. And so Paula flashed him a "This is it, Louie" look, gave a smart tug on his leash and *Voila!* they were on. By the time we (Geraldine and dogs) joined them, Louie was as at home on trams as if he were the conductor. Which goes to prove that dogs, like people, will adapt when they must—and often wind up enjoying themselves.

Try to avoid rush hours on public transportation, especially if you're a tourist. You'll have enough to do to watch out for your stop without worrying about your dog being stepped on or your animal's case being knocked about. Generally speaking, people would really rather not hurt an animal. But, as you may know from personal experience, our species tends to be cranky and preoccupied during rush hours. People may overlook even the largest dog, with unhappiness resulting on all sides. When you must travel in the crush, try to locate your pet where it won't be jostled. If there's not enough room for that, you'll simply have to keep a constant protective eye on your pet and risk missing your stop. That's life.

Animals, like ourselves, vary in their personal styles of traveling. Whenever it's permitted, Louie and Twiggy clamber up on a vacant tram, bus or train seat to enjoy the scenery and bask in the admiring glances and compliments of the other passengers. Lorenzo, perhaps because he's smaller, prefers peace and tranquillity under the seat. No one can predict just what *your* pet's style will be. You'll have to observe what makes it most comfortable and try to accommodate the animal when it's possible.

TRAVELING BY PLANE

Plane travel is the one situation we feel definitely calls for a tranquilizer for your pet . . . and, often, for yourself. It should receive medication no matter whether it's traveling in the cabin with you or in the baggage compartment.

Dogs take tranquilizers and cats take sedatives, but whichever it is, you should get it from a licensed veterinarian *only*. Most of us don't know beans about veterinary medicine and it's safer to let the vet prescribe. He knows what medication is appropriate according to your animal's weight, disposition and the length of time you'll be traveling. This is a good time to discuss how to vary the dosage should you prefer, as we do, to tranquilize your pet slightly for the trip to the airport and give it the remaining medicine just before flight time. (See page 30 for how to give tranquilizers.)

I (Geraldine) find it helpful to get the prescription a few days before we travel so that I can try out the recommended dosage on Twiggy and Lorenzo. In this way it's possible to observe for yourself how quickly the medication takes effect, just what that effect is and how long it lasts. And if it seems to be ineffective or inspires the wrong reaction in your pet, you have enough time to have the vet correct it.

Your pet can have a light meal 6 hours before the flight but it should have no food after that. Don't let it drink any water within 2 hours of the trip, unless the weather is extremely hot. If your trip will take 24 hours or more, outfit a plastic or mesh bag with food and water dishes, instructions and food . . . preferably dry, but canned is all right—if you include a can opener. Secure this bag to the kennel.

Take along some bedding for your pet's kennel and a sturdy, well-loved toy to keep the animal company. The toy should be hard, solid, unshreddable rubber without bells or other gadgets your pet might swallow or choke on. An exceptionally good choice for dogs is one of the edible rawhide toys that come in a variety of shapes and are sold in pet shops and supermarkets everywhere.

Be sure your pet is wearing an identification tag stating its name, destination, and your name and address. The kennel should be similarly tagged. If your animal bites or scratches, include that information.

Exercise your pet before flight time.

Some of these details will be dealt with more specifically in the sections on domestic and international air travel. But, for the sake of giving you a general picture here, we'll repeat some information:

Unless your pet is traveling in the cabin with you, it's a

good idea to arrive a half hour or even an hour in advance of the recommended check-in time. (If you're flying your pet as cargo, you'll have to get there 2 to 6 hours before.) You may yourself be a nervous traveler and simply need the extra time to feel secure. If you're buying a kennel at the airport, you may need the time to guarantee you'll get one. Reservation clerks always assure you there'll be one available, but the best-laid plans of mice and men, et cetera, et cetera. You might have forgotten to reserve one or they may have run short. Whatever . . . that little bit of extra time can make all the difference between being pleasantly excited or positively hysterical at the start of your trip.

On most airlines your pet will travel in the baggage compartment of the plane—a clean, comfortably ventilated, pressurized area that is maintained at the same temperature as your cabin. It may be a bit lonesome for your pet, but you have not consigned it to the bowels of hell. Despite this reassurance, it will be difficult for you to say good-by, even for a short trip. The only thing we can suggest is that you do it quickly. As soon as you get to the airport, tend to your pet's travel arrangements and then turn the animal over to your airline's personnel. It's really a kindness to you both to make your farewells fond but fast.

TRAVELING BY TRAIN

Train travel is very easy on you and your animal. You can usually keep your pet in the compartment with you or you can visit and care for it in the baggage car if it must ride there.

It *is* a good idea to go to the train station by yourself the day before your trip, especially if you're traveling where the geography and/or language is unfamiliar to you. Buy your tickets, make your space reservations and get all the necessary departure information. Also find out how long your train will be stopping at various stations en route so you can plan some exercise breaks for your pet.

Take along food, dishes, treats, a can opener and a knife. As far as we've observed, traveling by train doesn't affect your pet's appetite one whit. Therefore, be prepared to feed it dinner if your trip will take longer than a few hours. Always take a water bowl along.

TRAVEL TIPS FOR ANY OCCASION

No matter what means of transportation you're traveling by, the following rules usually apply:

Don't feed your pet for several hours in advance.

Don't give it water within 2 hours of traveling, unless the weather's very hot.

Always provide for water in transit.

Take along some things your animal is familiar with: toys, bedding, dishes.

Whenever possible let your pet get used to its traveling case in advance of a trip.

Be sure your pet is wearing identification—a tag with its name, destination, your name and address, and any information pertinent to locating you on your trip.

If your pet's traveling in a crate or kennel, write or tape the same information on the outside of the kennel.

Provide food and feeding equipment, and, when necessary, instructions, for a trip of any length.

Keep the animal's necessary documents with your own most important papers.

Exercise your pet before the trip.

WHEN *NOT* TO TRAVEL WITH YOUR PET

There are times when it's better for your animal to remain at home. Your pet should not travel if it's pregnant; old, feeble or terribly nervous; or when it's recovering from an illness. It's also wise to avoid taking your pet on a trip when she's in heat—she's likely to be very nervous *and* a magnet to males of her species. Your vet may be able to prescribe medication to minimize this particular estrus so that she's calmer and less beset by suitors. Bear in mind, however, this medication doesn't always work.

If you absolutely must travel when your animal's not in good shape, be sure to consult a veterinarian first as to what medication and arrangements will be safest for your pet.

YOUR PET'S BAGGAGE

Here are some items we've found useful to have along. You won't need *all* of them for *all* trips, so adapt freely. It helps to keep your animal's equipment in one handy place—a canvas shopping bag or a small lightweight travel case will do very well. Remember, most of these things are available wherever you go. If you forget anything, it's not likely to be a major catastrophe. But it's convenient to have:

—your pet's blanket or other favorite bedding
—toys to play with and chew on
—an old towel, in case you have to dry the animal off
—a thermos of water for car travel
—a can opener
—a knife
—dry food or packets of nonperishable meat for:
   (a) Sunday trips when stores might be closed
   (b) traveling in sparsely populated areas
   (c) long train trips
   (d) the first portion of your travels abroad. It helps to have some food from home while you're recuperating from "jet lag" and not up to coping with too many new things. When you're ready to shop for pet food, consult pages 234-50.

—2 plastic bowls for food and water

—grooming equipment—a comb and brush are usually sufficient

—a wallet-type case for your pet's documents if you want to be fancy, although it's probably better to carry them with your passport or driver's license

—this book, for its wealth of information

—a first-aid kit, although you can buy any of these or make adequate substitutes practically anywhere you go. But check the list to see what you'd feel better about having along. (Carry liquids in unbreakable bottles.)

    a rectal thermometer (might be useful abroad where centigrade thermometers may prove disconcerting)

    small milk of magnesia

    anti-diarrhea preparation

    a gentle commercial eyewash

    2" or 3" gauze bandage

    adhesive tape

    tweezers

    alcohol

    absorbent cotton

    aspirin

    mineral oil and Q-Tips for cleaning ears

    prescribed tranquilizers or sedatives

    extra prescriptions of any medication your pet is taking regularly

—a couple of packages of your pet's favorite treats, to reward it for being such a splendid traveler.

BASIC MEDICAL INFORMATION

It is our fond hope that you and your pet will enjoy splendid health during your travels and that, except for administering tranquilizers, you won't need this information at all.

How to Give Tranquilizers and Other Pills

I (Geraldine) have heard wonderful tales of people cleverly hiding a pill in their animal's food and the whole business is over with by dinner's end. But my dogs, and every cat of my acquaintance, can smell out subterfuge and the morsel containing the pill always remains on the plate. So I tackle the problem directly and here's how: With one hand, tilt your pet's head up and open its jaws. Try to have its upper lip curled somewhat over its teeth to prevent its biting down. With the other hand, quickly place the pill as far back and center on its tongue as you can comfortably manage. Quickly close its mouth and, keeping it closed, massage its throat gently for a few seconds to encourage swallowing. This usually works. It it doesn't and the pill is once again on the carpet before you while your pet gazes at you reproachfully, you will have to try again. However, to avoid the tedium and tension attendant on endless repetitions, follow the A.S.P.C.A.'s suggestion and for your next try coat the pill lightly with butter or oil.

How to Give Liquids

When medicine is in liquid form, first put a small quantity of it in a clean bowl and present it hopefully to your pet. If it's noxious to the animal—and it usually is—then call in an assistant. One of you should hold the animal firmly but gently while the other gives the medicine. Tilt your pet's head up. Gently pull out its lower lip where it forms a pocket with the upper lip. Trickle the medicine into this pocket slowly. It will wend its way between your pet's teeth and onto its tongue, at which point the animal will begin swallowing. Unless it's expressly forbidden, have some fresh water on hand for your animal to drink afterward.

This might be a somewhat messy procedure, so place your animal on newspaper beforehand. Also, you'll have a steadier hand and greater control over the flow of the medicine if you use a narrow-necked bottle or plastic medicine dropper instead of a spoon.

Your Animal's Temperature

The normal temperature for a dog or cat is 100.4° to 102.2° Fahrenheit or 38° to 39° centigrade.

Lubricate the bulb of a rectal thermometer with Vaseline and insert it gently into your animal's rectum. Hold the animal steady while you take the reading.

The Safety Muzzle

The A.S.P.C.A. recommends that you apply a safety muzzle when treating burns or wounds. clipping nails or giving liquid medicine to an unruly animal.

Take a long piece of gauze bandage or soft cloth, loop it in the middle and slip the loop around the animal's snout. Pull it tight, then bring the ends down and tie them under the animal's chin. Then draw the ends behind its ears and tie them into a bow resting right below the base of its skull. Speak reassuringly to your animal throughout this operation, and praise your pet when it's over.

Illness or Injury

The cardinal rule to observe whenever your animal is ill or injured is: Get the animal to a veterinarian as fast as possible.

You should, however, know what to do in extreme emergencies; you may be able to save your pet's life by acting swiftly.

Shock

Shock is extremely serious and requires immediate treatment. It can be caused by:
> exposure to extreme heat or cold
> loss of blood
> pain
> any trauma that severely damages tissue

The symptoms are:
> rapid shallow breathing
> subnormal temperature or the pet's body may feel cold
> semiconsciousness or total unconsciousness
> pallid mucous membranes and gums

Treatment:
> keep your animal's head lower than its body
> keep your pet warm
> don't give it anything to drink if it's unconscious
> feed the animal warm liquids if it's conscious enough to swallow
> form a pocket of its lip and slowly pour the liquid in if it's too weak to lap

Suffocation

This can be caused by:
> drowning
> smoke inhalation

If your pet has stopped breathing, give artificial respiration:
> place the animal on its right side
> see to it that its tongue is extended
> with a smooth, gentle, steady rhythm press your hands down on your pet's ribs for 5 seconds, then release for 5 seconds

alternate this press and release until your animal resumes
breathing

Bleeding

From an *artery*: the blood is bright red and spurts out
strongly.

Act fast or your pet may bleed to death. Apply pressure
directly on the severed artery:

> put your finger on the severed artery and press firmly
> until the bleeding stops

or

> apply a tourniquet. Tie a piece of cloth above the wound,
> on the side toward the heart. Insert a pencil or stick
> inside the loop formed by the knot. Turn the pencil
> until the bleeding stops. *Untwist the pencil and loosen
> the tourniquet every 8 minutes.*

From a *vein*: the blood is dark red and flows steadily. Put a
tight bandage on the wound.

Burns

Superficial burns: simply apply a generous amount of Vaseline.

Severe burns: restrain your animal from licking the burn
and get the animal to a veterinarian immediately.

Cuts and Scrapes

For deep punctures and large gashes, take your pet to a
veterinarian immediately.

For less severe cuts, gently wash the wound with soap and
water to clear away dirt and fur. Then apply a mild anti-
septic. If your pet keeps licking at the cut, then cover it with
a bandage.

Fracture

If your animal breaks a bone, try to get a veterinarian to come at once. Both your pet and the fractured area should be handled as little as possible.

An animal in pain is not going to behave reasonably, so apply a safety muzzle.

Treat your pet for shock, which it's likely to suffer—especially if the break is severe.

When you absolutely must move a seriously injured animal, the A.S.P.C.A. recommends that you apply a splint to the injury to prevent both ends of the bone from moving. You can make one out of any long, firm object, and any soft material will serve as padding. Tie the splint on firmly but not so tight that you cut off blood circulation.

Forget about the splint if your animal struggles because the movement might just cause greater injury.

If you must move a seriously injured animal, slide it carefully onto a board or strong piece of cardboard or a coat held taut. Get the animal to a veterinarian immediately.

Poisoning

This is another situation in which you must act really swiftly.

Unless your pet has swallowed an acid or an alkali, treat poisoning by inducing the animal to vomit. Two effective emetics that are readily available are:

    warm salt water

    soapsuds solution

You can also use a solution of mustard and water or half hydrogen peroxide and half water.

If your pet won't swallow, place a spoonful of salt way

back on its tongue, hold its mouth closed for a few seconds and stroke its throat to encourage swallowing.

If you know the poisoning was caused by an acid (nitric, sulfuric, etc.), *do not induce vomiting*. Neutralize with milk of magnesia or bicarbonate of soda. Follow this with milk or olive oil or egg white.

If the poison was an alkali, such as lye, soda, potash, *do not induce vomiting*. Give a neutralizing agent—vinegar or lemon juice and follow this with milk or olive oil or egg white.

There are many types of poisoning, so this list is confined to just those that might unluckily occur while traveling:

> sleeping pills, tranquilizers—induce vomiting and follow up with strong coffee
>
> spoiled food—induce vomiting, then give a mild laxative followed by an enema
>
> pesticides—just induce vomiting
>
> phosphorus from matches—induce vomiting and follow up with an Epsom salts solution
>
> iodine—induce vomiting and follow up with starch boiled in water
>
> lead paint—induce vomiting, follow up with an Epsom salts solution and then give milk or egg white

THESE
UNITED
STATES

WHAT TO EXPECT
ALONG THE WAY

Contrary to popular belief, it's an easy matter to travel with your pet anywhere in the United States except Hawaii. There's no language barrier to cope with; there's a staggering variety of pet food available throughout the country; pet shops, veterinarians and grooming services abound; and there are literally hundreds of hotels and motels that welcome pets.

Why assume that you must go through the expense and lonesomeness of boarding your pet when vacationtime rolls around? United States rules simply *aren't* that strict, and you'll find that it's usually cheaper and certainly a great deal more fun to take your pet along.

In fact, we firmly believe that most vacation plans would be greatly enhanced by including your pet. Consider, for example, a visit to a large American city. Our cities are very complex and, while there is a great deal to see, even the most enthusiastic tourist may be beset by a sense of isolation and disorientation. Your cat—that adaptable, easy-to-care-for animal—can impart a feeling of home to even the most impersonal hotel room. Your dog, too, is a definite asset not only as a companion but as a great socializer. Conversations with other people just seem to happen naturally when there's a dog around, which is a marvelous antidote to feeling lonely in a big city.

As John Steinbeck's *Travels with Charley* amply illustrates, a cross-country tour is a special pleasure in the company of your pet, and a camping trip is an absolute natural for your dog or cat.

Now you may well agree with us that it would be *fun* to take your pet along but is it really possible? This chapter shows you how very possible it is. We will discuss general rules regarding animals and specific state regulations pertaining to their entry. Hopefully, by the end of this chapter, you will abandon any fears you might have had, and you and your pet will set forth with carefree hearts to explore these United States.

IN GENERAL

Public transport, such as intracity buses, subways and streetcars, generally requires your animal to be in a carrying case that you can hold or place under your seat. On ferries and in small cities and towns, your dog may be merely leashed or leashed and muzzled.

One word about muzzles: It's a good idea to *carry* one with you. But don't make your dog wear one unless it's absolutely necessary for local law or your dog's disposition. If you muzzle your dog just to be "on the safe side" of the law, you not only make your dog uncomfortable but people then get the impression that your dog is vicious. This only encourages needless fear and makes it tougher on all of us, dogs and owners alike.

Some boards of health—New York City's, for instance—take a dim view toward pets being in any place where food is sold or served. Therefore, you're not likely to be sharing dining-out experiences with your pet unless you go to a drive-in restaurant or are in a rural or casual area. Americans are notoriously fond of animals, however, and if a restaurateur can't allow your pet to sit in the dining area with you, he will probably arrange some comfortable place for your animal to wait in.

You can take your pet shopping in large department stores throughout the country. Small stores sometimes forbid animals but this depends on the personal feelings of the shopkeeper. Most do allow you to bring your animal in as long as it's well behaved and doesn't knock everything over. Outdoor markets and auctions also allow pets.

Dogs are expected to be leashed and curbed when out walking in cities. For all our sakes, it's a good policy to curb your dog wherever you are. Dogs are permitted in most parks and often there will be an area designated by custom or regulation where they may run free. If you let your pet run loose in any other area, just be sure you have its leash handy. In some cities, such as New York, there are periodic police patrols and you can wind up with a fine if your dog is not swiftly leashed. There's no need to be tense about it though. By some telepathic consent your fellow park strollers will send out an "early warning" so that rarely, if ever, are you taken unaware.

Museums do not permit pets nor do movie theaters—unless you go to a drive-in cinema or your pet is so small it's able to enter unnoticed.

"Pet sitters" are always available and charge slightly less than baby-sitting rates. If you'd like your dog taken for a romp in the park while you visit a museum, ask the personnel at your hotel. They will either have someone on the staff or will know a local person who will gladly help you out.

STATE ENTRY REGULATIONS

Most of the states do require some documented assurance of your animal's health. Whether or not you're ever asked for it depends largely upon your means of transport and the amount of curiosity your animal inspires. Gilbert, a friend of Paula's, toured the United States by car in the company of Troilus and Cressida, two Great Danes—scarcely an inconspicuous duo—and yet wasn't once asked for their papers. Most of you have had some experience traveling interstate by car. You know then that you are rarely, if ever, stopped. It is highly unlikely that you will be asked for your pet's papers unless there's been a recent rabies scare or you are motoring with a chimpanzee or a pet cougar.

We are eager to introduce a note of realism into this matter of health documents that, at first glance, seems so formidable to most of us. If you are traveling by plane or by train, then pay very strict attention to your destination state's requirements. Life is more casual when you are traveling by car, and if your pet is wearing its rabies vaccination tag, that will generally suffice.

The Health Certificate

The basic document required is a health certificate, made out on official stationery by an accredited licensed veterinarian in your state of origin . . . that means your regular vet, who's done this a million times.

The certificate should state the following information:
(a) your name and address
(b) your pet's name, species and breed
(c) if you are shipping your pet to someone else, give the name and address of the person you're sending it to
(d) that your pet is free from and has not been exposed to any infectious or contagious disease
(e) that your pet does not come from a rabies-quarantined area or an area where rabies is known to exist
(f) depending on your animal's age, the date rabies vaccination was administered and what type of vaccine

was used, and as a bonus, the serial number of your
pet's vaccination tag

If your pet is a psittacine bird, the certificate must declare
that your bird is free from and has not been exposed to
psittacosis.

Some states require that this health certificate be stamped
by the official seal of the federal veterinarian for your state.
Unless we mention it, however, your personal veterinarian's
signature is sufficient. If your situation is such that you must
meet this requirement, just mail the certificate to your federal
veterinarian (see pages 160-63), who will promptly return
it properly stamped.

Types of Pets

Naturally, not all of us have the same kinds of pets. If you
have a Siamese cat, there's no need to bother your head about
the rules on marmoset monkeys and vice versa. To simplify
matters, the requirements are listed by categories of animals.
We are following the U.S. Department of Agriculture's defini-
tions for those categories. If there are no requirements listed
for *your* pet's category, that means there are none in that
particular state.

Dogs and *Cats* mean those domestic animals we all know
and love so well. But under *Dogs* you'll occasionally see ex-
emptions for exhibition, performance or breeding dogs and
we'd like to clarify those terms. Exhibition = dog show; performance = circus or other theatrical activity; breeding =
what can we say? . . . when you've sent your dog to a kennel for stud purposes.

Birds—Psittacine birds such as parrots, parakeets, lovebirds,
cockatoos, budgerigars, Amazons, African grays, macaws,
parrotlets, lories, lorikeets, beebees—in short, *only* those
birds susceptible to psittacosis.

Wild—Wild and semiwild animals you're as likely to meet in your native woods as in a pet shop: i.e., rabbits, beavers, raccoons, mice, rats, guinea pigs, hamsters, skunks and porcupines.

Zoo—Monkeys, baboons, chimpanzees, lemurs, marmosets, cheetahs, pumas, cougars, leopards—those exotic creatures more apt to be seen in a zoo than in someone's home.

The rulings governing cattle, swine, sheep, goats, horses and poultry are so extensive that if you have any such animal for a pet, we suggest you write the U.S. Department of Agriculture, Animal Health Division, Federal Center Building, Hyattsville, Maryland 20782. They'll send you their booklet ARS 91-17-5 entitled "State-Federal Health Requirements and Regulations Governing the Interstate and International Movement of Livestock and Poultry."

REQUIREMENTS BY STATE

ALABAMA

Dogs   Health certificate.
         If older than 3 months, proof of rabies vaccination not more than 6 months prior to entry.
         No dog is admitted if infested with screwworms.

Wild   Health certificate.
& Zoo If you plan on staying, notify the federal veterinarian for Alabama (see page 161) within 10 days after entry so that he may arrange an immediate examination of your pet. No animal infested with screwworms is permitted entry.

ALASKA

Dogs   Health certificate (valid for only 30 days).

Proof of rabies vaccination not more than 6 months prior to entering Alaska.

ARIZONA

Considers health certificates invalid after 30 days of issuance.

Dogs   Health certificate.

If 4 months or older, need proof of rabies vaccination: killed-virus vaccine—within 12 months prior to entry.

Live-virus vaccine—within 36 months prior to entry.

Birds   Must have a certificate stating they've undergone the 45-day treatment with chlortetracycline (see federal import requirements on page 269).

Wild   Health certificate.

If you plan on staying, contact the Arizona Game & Fish Department, 1680 West Adams Street, Phoenix, Arizona 85007.

ARKANSAS

Dogs   Health certificate.

Proof of rabies vaccination within 12 months of entry.

Cats   Health certificate.

Proof of rabies vaccination within 12 months of entry.

Wild   Health certificate.

CALIFORNIA

Dogs   Health certificate.

If more than 4 months old, proof of rabies vaccination:

nerve-tissue vaccine—within 12 months of entry.

chick-embryo vaccine—within 24 months of entry.

Cats   Your cat can freely enjoy the California sunshine just as long as it seems in good health.

Birds   Health certificate.

Wild Birds or Animals

> There are no restrictions on bringing in monkeys, chimpanzees or other common *zoo* animals. But if your pet should be a "bird, mammal, frog, toad, salamander, bony fish, lamprey, reptile, crayfish, slug or snail which is not normally domesticated or native to California" you will have to apply for an entry permit to the California Department of Fish and Game, 1416 Ninth Street, Sacramento, California 95814.

COLORADO

Dogs Health certificate.

> If 3 months or older, proof of rabies vaccination not less than 30 days or more than 6 months prior to entry.

Cats Health certificate.

Birds Health certificate recommended.

Wild No skunks may be brought into Colorado.

CONNECTICUT

Dogs & Cats You don't need a thing if your pet is in Connecticut for exhibition purposes or if your visit is for 21 days or less. Otherwise, you need a health/rabies certificate.

Wild If yours is a potentially dangerous animal, you will be liable for any damage it causes. If you are vacationing or planning to take up residence in Connecticut, you must obtain a permit for your animal from the chief executive authority in the town you're staying in.

DELAWARE

Dogs Health certificate.

> If older than 4 months, proof of rabies vaccination.

Cats   Health certificate.
Wild   Health certificate.

DISTRICT OF COLUMBIA
        No requirements listed for any pet.

FLORIDA
        In general, Florida's policy is "seeing is believing."
Dogs   Health certificate.
        Proof of rabies vaccination within 6 months of entry.
        Dogs visiting for exhibition purposes are exempt.
Cats, Birds, Wild & Zoo
        Need only be free of evidence of contagious or infectious diseases, should they be examined.

GEORGIA
Dogs   Health certificate.
        If 3 months or older, proof of rabies vaccination within 6 months of entry. They should also wear their tags.
Birds   You may have up to 4 psittacine birds with you as pets while vacationing in or traveling through Georgia.

HAWAII
    All *Dogs, Cats & Other Carnivores* will be held in quarantine for 120 days upon arrival in Hawaii. You will have to pay a $5 registration fee for each animal and $1.20 for every day of quarantine for your dog and 90 cents per day for your cat. You may visit your pet weekdays from 3 P.M. to 5 P.M. and Saturdays and Sundays from 1 P.M. to 3 P.M. The quarantine station is closed on holidays. If your animal is ill, you will have to bear the expense for its treatment. Payment of the quarantine fees can be arranged on an installment basis if they prove financially difficult for you.

IDAHO

Dogs

If 4 months or older, proof of rabies vaccination:
nerve-tissue vaccine—within 6 months of entry.
chick-embryo vaccine—within 24 months of entry.

If your puppy is from a rabies-quarantined area and
has not been inoculated against rabies, you will
need a permit for him from the Bureau of Animal
Industry, P.O. Box 7249, Boise, Idaho 83707.
Telephone: (208) 344-5811, extension 465.

ILLINOIS

Dogs   Health certificate.

If 4 months or older, proof of rabies vaccination:
killed-virus vaccine—within 6 months of entry.
live-virus vaccine—within 12 months of entry.

Your dog is exempt from these requirements if it is in
Illinois a limited time for performance, exhibition
or breeding purposes and is under direct control
while visiting.

Wild   No San Juan, alias European, rabbits are permitted
entry for any reason whatsoever.

If you wish to set free either your pet or its young,
you will first need permission from the Director of
the Illinois Department of Conservation, 102 State
Office Building, Springfield 62706. Telephone: (217)
525-6424.

INDIANA

Dogs   Health certificate.

If 3 months or older, proof of rabies vaccination with
modified live-virus vaccine only within 1 year of
entry.

Cats   Health certificate.

If 4 months or older, proof of rabies vaccination (any
type) within 1 year of entry.

Make sure your pet has plenty of room.

If your animal originates from a rabies-quarantined area, you must obtain special permission from the Indiana federal veterinarian (see page 160) before bringing it in.

IOWA

Dogs   Health certificate.

If 3 months or older, proof of rabies vaccination:
modified live-virus (chick-embryo) vaccine—within 2 years of entry.
killed-virus (caprine) vaccine—within 1 year of entry.

Exhibition and performing dogs are exempt from these requirements.

KANSAS

Dogs   Health certificate.

If 3 months or older, proof of rabies vaccination within 12 months of entry.

Cats, Wild & Zoo
Health certificate.

KENTUCKY

Dogs   Health certificate.

If 4 months or older, proof of rabies vaccination:
killed-virus vaccine—within 12 months of entry.
modified live-virus vaccine—within 24 months of entry.

Exhibition and performing dogs are exempt if they will not be in Kentucky more than 10 days.

Cats   Health certificate.

If 4 months or older, proof of rabies vaccination with killed-virus vaccine within 12 months of entry.

Wild   Health certificate or a permit. Permits are obtainable
& Zoo   from the Department of Fish and Wildlife Resources, State Office Building Annex, Frankfort, Kentucky 40601. Telephone: (502) 564-3400.

If you're planning on staying in Kentucky, they'd like you to notify Dr. L. G. Northington, State Veterinarian, within 10 days. He's at the Division of Livestock Sanitation, Department of Agriculture, New Capitol Annex, Frankfort, Kentucky 40601. He will arrange an examination to further certify your animal's health.

LOUISIANA

Dogs   Health certificate.
If older than 2 months, proof of rabies immunization:
nerve-tissue vaccine—within 12 months of entry.
chick-embryo vaccine—within 24 months of entry.

Wild
& Zoo   Need only be reported to the Louisiana federal veterinarian (see page 162) within 10 days of entry, so if you're just passing through, you have nothing to worry about.

MAINE

If you're planning a vacation in Maine, you can breathe a sigh of relief.

Dogs
& Cats   There are no entrance requirements.

Wild
& Zoo   Need a permit, easily obtainable by writing to the Department of Inland Fisheries and Game, State Office Building, Augusta, Maine 04330.

MARYLAND

Maryland requires that your pet's health certificate be further certified by the federal veterinarian for your state (see page 162).

Dogs   Health certificate.
If 4 months or older, proof of at least 1 rabies vaccination within 12 months of entry.

Cats   Health certificate.

Birds   Health certificate.

Wild   Maryland would like you to report their presence
           within 72 hours of entry into the state to the
           Maryland State Board of Agriculture, Livestock
           Sanitary Service, Symons Hall, University of Mary-
           land, College Park, Maryland 20742.

MASSACHUSETTS

Dogs   Health certificate.
           Proof of rabies vaccination within 12 months of entry.
           Exhibition dogs are exempt.

Birds   Health certificate.

MICHIGAN

Dogs   Your dog's health certificate must be approved by the
           federal veterinarian for your state (see pages 160-
           63).
           It must state that your dog has been vaccinated
           against rabies within 6 months of entry.
           Any unvaccinated dog or one originating from a
           rabies-quarantined area is subject to a 60-day quar-
           antine.

Rabbits No live San Juan, alias European, rabbit is permitted
           entry for any purpose.

MINNESOTA

Dogs   Health certificate.
           Proof of rabies vaccination:
               killed-virus vaccine—within 12 months of entry.
               modified live-virus vaccine—within 24 months of
                   entry.
           Performing dogs are exempt.
           Dogs originating from a rabies-quarantined area
           need a permit from the Minnesota Livestock Sani-

tary Board Office, 555 Wabasha Street, St. Paul,
Minnesota 55102. Their telephone is (612) 221-
2741 and they can be reached 24 hours a day, 7
days a week.

MISSISSIPPI

Dogs   Health certificate.

If 3 months or older, proof of rabies vaccination
within 6 months of entry.

MISSOURI

Dogs   Health certificate *issued within 15 days of entry*.

If 4 months or older, proof of rabies vaccination:
killed-virus vaccine—within 1 year of entry.
modified live-virus vaccine—within 2 years of entry.

Dogs visiting for performance, exhibition or breeding
purposes are exempt if their stay does not exceed
30 days and if they are kept leashed.

MONTANA

Dogs   Health certificate.

If 3 months or older, proof of rabies vaccination with
modified live-virus vaccine within 2 years of entry.

Dogs originating from a rabies-quarantined area will
need a written permit from the federal veterinarian for Montana (see page 161).

NEBRASKA

Dogs   Health certificate.

If 4 months or older, proof of rabies vaccination:
killed-virus vaccine (caprine)—not less than 21
days or more than 1 year prior to entry.
modified live-virus vaccine (chick embryo)—not
less than 21 days or more than 2 years prior to
entry.

NEVADA

Dogs Health certificate.

If 4 months or older, proof of rabies vaccination:
nerve-tissue vaccine—within 12 months of entry.
chick-embryo vaccine—within 24 months of entry.

If you're just passing through or your dog is in Nevada for performance purposes, the above requirements do not apply. Dogs originating from rabies-quarantined areas need a permit before entering the state, from the Director, Division of Animal Industry, Nevada State Department of Agriculture, P.O. Box 1209, Reno, 89504. Telephone: (702) 784-6401.

Psittacine, Exotic and Wild Birds; Zoo, Wild and Semiwild Animals

Need permission to enter from the Nevada State Fish and Game Commission, 1100 Valley Road, Reno, Nevada 89502. Telephone: (702) 784-6214.

NEW HAMPSHIRE

Dogs Health certificate.

If 3 months or older, proof of rabies vaccination:
killed-virus vaccine—within 1 year of entry.
live-virus vaccine—within 3 years of entry.

NEW JERSEY

Dogs Health certificate bearing proof of rabies vaccination.

Birds Health certificate must also state that they originate from an area free of psittacosis. Otherwise, a special permit must be obtained from the Bureau of Veterinary Public Health, New Jersey Department of Health, P.O. Box 1540, Trenton, New Jersey 08607.

Wild Need a health certificate (valid for only 30 days).
& Zoo

NEW MEXICO

Dogs   Health certificate.

If 4 months or older, proof of rabies vaccination within 12 months of entry.

NEW YORK

Wonder of wonders . . . there are no regulations as of this writing for any pet!

NORTH CAROLINA

Dogs   Health certificate.

Proof of rabies vaccination within 12 months of entry and a statement that they've not been exposed to rabies within 100 days of entry.

Dogs entering from rabies-quarantined areas need a permit from the federal veterinarian for North Carolina (see page 162).

Wild   Should be reported as to their number and kind within 10 days of entry to the federal veterinarian for North Carolina (see page 162).

The animal(s) must be available for examination.

NORTH DAKOTA

Dogs   Health certificate stating no exposure to rabies within 100 days of entry.

If 4 months or older, proof of rabies vaccination with one of the modified live-virus vaccines within 3 years of entry.

Exhibition dogs are exempt.

Hunting dogs must have proof of rabies vaccination not less than 30 days prior to entry.

OHIO

Dogs   Health certificate.

If 6 months or older, proof of rabies vaccination:

chick-embryo vaccine—within 3 years of entry.
other vaccines—within 1 year of entry.
Performing dogs are exempt.

OKLAHOMA
Dogs Health certificate.
Proof of rabies vaccination:
nerve-tissue vaccine—within 1 year of entry.
modified live-virus vaccine—within 2 years of entry.

OREGON
Dogs Health certificate.
If 4 months or older, proof of rabies vaccination:
killed-virus vaccine—within 6 months of entry.
modified live-virus vaccine—within 2 years of entry.
Cats Health certificate.
Wild Need a permit from the federal veterinarian for
& Zoo Oregon (see page 163).

PENNSYLVANIA
Dogs Health certificate stating no exposure to rabies within 100 days of entry.
Performance, exhibition and breeding dogs are exempt if their stay for those purposes does not exceed 30 days.

RHODE ISLAND
Dogs Health certificate.
Proof of rabies vaccination:
killed-virus vaccine—not less than 30 days or more than 6 months prior to entry.
modified live-virus vaccine—within 2 years of entry.

Birds   These regulations apply only if you are *shipping* your birds into Rhode Island. You send your birds' health certificates plus a statement as to the number and kinds of birds to be imported and the origin, date and destination of the shipment to the Chief, Division of Animal Industry, Rhode Island Department of Health. Ask him for a permit, which he will mail back to you.

SOUTH CAROLINA
Dogs   Health certificate.
          Proof of rabies vaccination within 12 months of entry.
Cats   Health certificate.
Birds   Health certificate.
Wild   Health certificate.
& Zoo

SOUTH DAKOTA
Dogs   Health certificate.
          If 3 months or older, proof of rabies vaccination within 1 year.
Cats   Health certificate.
          If 3 months or older, proof of rabies vaccination within 1 year.

TENNESSEE
Dogs   Health certificate.
          Proof of rabies vaccination, plus tag, showing inoculation within 1 year of entry.

TEXAS
Dogs   Health certificate.
          Proof of rabies vaccination within 6 months of entry.

UTAH

Dogs   Health certificate.

If more than 4 months old, proof of rabies vaccination:

killed-virus vaccine—within 1 year of entry.

modified live-virus vaccine—within 2 years of entry.

Cats   Health certificate.

If 4 months or older, proof of rabies vaccination:

killed-virus vaccine—within 1 year of entry.

modified live-virus vaccine—within 2 years of entry.

Birds   You need a permit only if you are *shipping* your birds into Utah. Write to the federal veterinarian for Utah (see page 163) requesting a permit and stating the number and kinds of birds you're shipping, their origin, date of shipment and destination. Also send along a health certificate.

Wild   Health certificate.
& Zoo

VERMONT

Dogs   Health certificate.

If 4 months or older, proof of rabies vaccination with modified live-virus vaccine within 1 year of entry.

Cats   Health certificate.

If 4 months or older, proof of rabies vaccination with modified live-virus vaccine within 1 year of entry.

Birds   Health certificate.

If you're shipping your birds into Vermont, they will be quarantined for 15 days and then examined by a state veterinarian who will then issue a health certificate.

Wild   You must first obtain permission to import your pet into Vermont from the Vermont Fish and Game Department, Montpelier, Vermont 05602.

VIRGINIA

Dogs   Health certificate.

If 4 months or older, proof of rabies vaccination, including tags, issued within 1 year of entry.

These regulations do not apply if you're just passing through or planning to make your home in Virginia.

Cats   Health certificate.

If 4 months or older, proof of rabies vaccination within 1 year of entry.

Again, these rules don't apply if you are just passing through Virginia or intend to make your home there.

Monkeys This includes all monkeys and subhuman primates.*
Health certificate.

A separate statement from your veterinarian declaring he has examined the oral mucosa of your pet and found no evidence of disease lesions or inflammatory processes.

A certificate stating that your pet has successfully passed a tuberculin test within 30 days of entry. This certificate should also state the kind and amount of tuberculin used, the date and hour of injection, the date and hour of observation following the injection, and that no response of any kind or degree was observed.

WASHINGTON

Dogs   Health certificate.

If 4 months or older, proof of rabies vaccination:

* These documents are not necessary for any monkey just passing through Virginia.

          killed-virus vaccine—within 6 months of entry.

          modified live-virus vaccine—within 2 years of entry.

Cats   Health certificate.

          If 4 months or older, proof of rabies vaccination:

          killed-virus vaccine—within 6 months of entry.

          modified live-virus vaccine—within 2 years of entry.

          Any animal originating from a rabies-quarantined area must have a permit obtained in advance of entry from the State Department of Agriculture in Olympia, Washington.

Birds Whether you ship or just bring your psittacine birds into Washington, you must obtain prior approval from the Washington State Department of Health, Smith Tower, Seattle, Washington 98104.

Wild   Need a permit from the State Department of Agri-
& Zoo culture in Olympia, Washington.

WEST VIRGINIA

If you *ship* your *Dog* or *Cat* into West Virginia, you must send a copy of its health certificate to the Director, Animal Health Division, State Department of Agriculture, State Capitol Building, Charleston, West Virginia 25305.

Dogs   Health certificate.

          Proof of rabies vaccination within 1 year of entry.

Cats   Health certificate.

          Proof of rabies vaccination within 1 year of entry.

Birds If you *ship* your birds in, you must first get a permit from the West Virginia State Department of Health, Division of Disease Control at the above address. Tell them the number and kinds of birds and the name and address of the consignee.

Wild   You are not permitted to let your animal run loose.

Keep it leashed or otherwise controlled at all times.

Zoo   You are not allowed to liberate any pet in this category either. In addition, your animal should have an interstate health certificate approved by the federal veterinarian of your state (see pages 160-63). Send a copy of this certificate to the Director, Animal Health Division at the above address.

WISCONSIN

Dogs   Health certificate.
   If 6 months or older, proof of rabies vaccination:
      chick-embryo vaccine—within 3 years of entry.
      other vaccines—within 1 year of entry.

WYOMING

Dogs   Health certificate.
   If older than 4 months, proof of rabies vaccination:
      nerve-tissue vaccine—within 1 year of entry.
      chick-embryo vaccine—within 2 years of entry.

HOW TO GET THERE

Getting there *can* be half the fun of traveling with your pet. In this section we hope to give you a clear idea of the costs, rulings and procedures involved in ordinary transportation—cars, bikes, buses, trains and planes—so that you and your pet will have a very pleasant trip.

BY AUTOMOBILE

If you're traveling in your own car, who's to stop you from taking your pet? Fortunately, you have the same freedom if you're renting a car. Car-rental agencies have no specific rulings on animal companions. They do, usually, have a clause in their contracts that states that you're financially liable for any damage done to their car while it's in your possession.

Theoretically, if your cat scratches up the seats, you'll have to pay the damages, but that will be covered by your insurance, and besides, *your* cat's not going to scratch the seats.

BY BICYCLE

Happily, bicycles are once again coming into favor, even in large cities. If yours is a small dog, it can fit quite comfortably into a bicycle basket, and you're off for a spin in the park!

BY BUS

Transcontinental bus companies, such as Greyhound and Continental Trailways, are prohibited by the Interstate Commerce Commission from carrying pets. (The only exception made is for a properly harnessed, muzzled Seeing Eye dog.) Now here is a law we should lobby against! It's understandable that they would forbid pets in the buses' baggage compartments. There, sure enough, pets would die from either carbon-monoxide poisoning or overexposure to heat or cold, depending on the season. But it's unreasonable to forbid small "hand luggage" pets on board . . . or even larger animals when there are few other passengers. Considering that buses are the cheapest and often the only means of transportation in many areas, this ruling imposes a form of economic discrimination. People are forced either to use more expensive transport or to stay at home. It's especially difficult now that we have fewer trains that can carry pets in the baggage cars. Since pets are rarely permitted in coaches, the only alternative left is private or semiprivate compartments . . . and that's not traveling on a shoestring! The next time you're in a letter-writing mood, drop the I.C.C. a little note of protest!

The rulings on intercity and intracity buses vary considerably. Frequently it's left to the driver's discretion as to whether you'll be allowed to take your animal. And no one can predict human nature. You are usually allowed to take a pet if it can qualify as hand luggage—that is, if it's in a case that you can hold on your lap or place under your seat. But that's flexible, too. On one New York–New Jersey trip, I (Geraldine) arrived at the bus terminal without a case and fortunately a very tolerant bus driver allowed me to carry 20-pound Twiggy on board in a paper shopping bag.

BY TRAIN

Railroads have all sorts of private accommodations now—Pullman, budget rooms, roomettes, slumber coaches, and so forth. And, generally speaking, they will let you take your animal into such a compartment with you. You must, however, keep your pet either in its carrier or leashed and muzzled while getting on and off the train. And you can't take your animal anywhere else except into your compartment. If you're sharing accommodations with people, your pet must be on its best behavior.

There is generally no charge for animals traveling in a compartment with you.

Take along enough food and treats for the trip, and take your pet's food and water dishes; train travel does not affect a pet's digestion, as far as we've noticed. Also, ask the conductor at which stops there'll be the longest waits so that you can take advantage of them to exercise your animal.

Baggage Car

You may find that the train you want to travel on has been affected by the personnel shortage and has converted to sealed baggage cars. In that instance, you must plan on private accommodations.

The railways that can still carry your pet in their baggage cars will allow you to visit your animal en route in order to give it its food and water. They rarely have personnel who can care for your pet for you.

Choose a sturdy, well-ventilated, easily handled crate or

kennel for your pet, and be sure to have food supplies and dishes along. Also, make sure you tape your pet's health documents to the kennel and write down all the necessary identification information on the outside of the kennel in big bold letters.

When you arrive at your destination, claim your animal immediately. The railroads have no facilities for your animal to wait in or be cared for. If you're shipping it alone, make extra sure that *someone* will be there to meet the train and claim the animal.

Just like parcel post, the cost for your pet to travel in the baggage car depends on the distance the pet is going. The price will be figured on the basis of the combined weight of your pet plus its kennel multiplied by the distance rate. The minimum weight is placed at 50 pounds and the minimum charge is $1. If you take your pet with you in the compartment but leave its crate in baggage, you'll be charged for the crate at the same distance rates multiplied by its weight. Again, the minimum charge is $1.

ATSF—ATCHISON, TOPEKA & SANTA FE

Coach passengers must place pets (except Seeing Eye dogs) in *baggage* service. *Sleeping car* passengers may take dogs, cats or other pets (provided they're not venomous, odoriferous or otherwise objectionable) into a private room, but not more than 2 animals are allowed in any one room. General regulations for baggage and private room apply.

BALTIMORE & OHIO

Small dogs are permitted in *coaches,* if not offensive to other passengers. Dogs, cats and other pets (if not objectionable) are permitted in *private* accommodations. There's a limit of 2 animals per room. Pets are not permitted in any other section of the train.

Burlington Northern

No baggage car facilities. Pets are permitted in the *sleeping car* or *slumber coach* sections. Pets must be leashed and muzzled or in a suitable carrier.

Central Railroad Company of New Jersey

This short-haul commuter railroad permits small animals in a carrier to remain with their owners during the trip.

Chesapeake & Ohio

Small dogs in containers are permitted in *coaches.* Dogs, cats and other animals (provided they're not objectionable) are permitted in *private rooms* but there must not be more than 2 animals in any one room. Animals must be in suitable containers to and from rooms; dogs may be leashed and muzzled. Animals are not permitted in any other section of the train.

Chicago, Rock Island & Pacific

Baggage cars are available only between Chicago and Peoria and Chicago and Rock Island. Otherwise, dogs, cats and other nonobjectionable pets may be taken into *private room* accommodations in sleeping cars. Only 2 animals per room are permitted. Pets must be in a suitable container when going to and from room, except for dogs that may instead be leashed and muzzled. Animals are not permitted in any other part of the train. One further stipulation: You must discourage your pet from barking or creating a disturbance to other passengers, otherwise your pet will be transferred to the baggage car.

Chicago South Shore & South Bend

Baggage car only for dogs, cats and other pets.

Delaware & Hudson

The rules for *baggage cars* are the same as in general regulations (page 63); any crate of pets or empty crates valued at more than $25 will be accepted if the owner pays $1 per $100 or fraction thereof. Pets are allowed in *sleeping car* accommodations, per usual. On the Long Island Railroad division, your pet must travel in a carrier and you will be charged $1 for each pet you bring on board.

Denver & Rio Grande Western

No pets.

Erie Lackawanna

This is essentially a commuter line and it does permit small pets in carriers to travel with their owners. Dogs too large to be carried may be muzzled instead but, in these instances, whether or not they'll be permitted is left up to the conductor.

Grand Trunk Western Railroad

Pets are permitted in the *baggage car only*. General rules apply.

Gulf, Mobile & Ohio

Sleeping car passengers are permitted to keep their pets with them. Other passengers must place their pets in *baggage,* feed and water them en route, and claim them immediately at their destination. It's possible to insure your animal beyond the railroad's liability of $25. You may purchase additional insurance up to $275 at $1 for each $100 or fraction thereof.

Illinois Central

Coach passengers must place their pets in *baggage,* according to the usual procedure and rates.

Pullman passengers may keep their pets with them at a cost of one-fifth of a first-class adult fare.

LONG ISLAND RAILROAD

See Delaware & Hudson.

LOUISVILLE & NASHVILLE

Small pets are permitted in *coaches* if they are in a basket or some other container.

MISSOURI PACIFIC

No pets.

PENN CENTRAL

Dogs, cats and other animals in traveling cases are permitted in *coaches* but not reserved-seat coaches or Metroliners or Turboservice trains. Seeing Eye dogs must be properly harnessed and muzzled and they are permitted in either *private compartments* or in the *baggage car*.

PORT AUTHORITY TRANS-HUDSON (PATH)

Pets must remain with their owner and be in a secure container. Any pet that cannot be so caged may be carried on PATH only if advance permission is obtained from Mr. L. D. Schwalb, Supervisor, Passenger Services, The Port of New York Authority, 111 Eighth Avenue, New York City 10011. Telephone: (212) 620-8221. Mr. Schwalb will determine whether your pet may travel, and how and when it will travel.

READING

Small pets are permitted to travel with their owners in *coaches* provided they're kept in suitable carriers and do not take up aisle or seat space.

Seaboard Coast Line

Pets may travel in *baggage cars* and their owners may visit to feed and look after them. Only Seeing Eye dogs are permitted in *coaches*. *Sleeping car* passengers may keep their pets with them free of charge. Pets must be leashed and muzzled or in suitable containers.

Southern Pacific

No baggage facilities. Pets are allowed in *sleeping car* compartments *only*. A carrier is not necessary and there is no charge.

Southern Railway

At the time this book was being written, the Southern Railway was debating whether or not to continue allowing small pets in baskets or other suitable cases to travel with *coach* passengers. We suggest you check to see what the current regulation on this is. Pets are permitted in *private compartments* or may travel in the *baggage car*, as per usual.

Union Pacific

Pets are permitted in *private compartments* or may travel in the *baggage car*.

BY PLANE

When you make your reservation, inform your airline that your pet will be coming along for the ride. If they sell kennels and you need one, ask them to reserve one for you in the appropriate size at the airport check-in counter. If you're taking your own kennel, tell them its size so they can figure it into their baggage calculations and save space for your pet. Try to make your reservation two or three days in advance if it's possible.

Build a proper sized box for your pet.

Most airlines will not permit animals, except for Seeing Eye dogs, in the cabin of the plane. Of the few that do, Pan Am and TWA try their best to keep the seat next to you vacant—that gives you and your pet more room *and* it avoids annoying other passengers. There's a limit though on how many animals may travel in the cabin, so make your reservation early to be sure *your* pet's the lucky one.

There's a limit, too, on what size animal may travel in the cabin. Cats and small and toy dogs are the only candidates considered.

Your animal will have to take some tranquilizing medication for plane travel, and for advice on this and what else you should do to prepare it for the trip, we suggest you read pages 24-26.

When taking your own kennel, make sure it's superstrong, has a leakproof bottom, and is so constructed that your pet cannot hurt itself on sharp edges or protrusions. The airlines will not permit your animal to travel in anything that does not meet these standards.

If you're shipping your pet as air freight, you must take it to your airline's air-freight office 2 to 6 hours in advance of the flight. Check with the cargo people a day before so they will know to prepare for your animal. The cargo office is often at a considerable distance from your airline's terminal counter. If you're unfamiliar with the airport—and why shouldn't you be?—ask them their exact location and get directions on how best to get there.

When your pet is traveling on the same flight as yourself, most airlines handle its arrangements at the normal check-in counter. They suggest you arrive a half hour before the scheduled check-in time. We suggest you arrive an hour before, especially if you're buying a kennel or have one that you have to put together. It has been known to happen that even a normally efficient airline has forgotten to reserve the kennel you need and there's a wild scramble all over the terminal while they try to get one from another airline. Or it might happen that the kennel they've reserved is more appropriate for a house mouse than for your cocker spaniel. Little surprises such as these require extra time to cope with —and to recuperate from—so do yourself a favor and get there early.

Most important of all, if you're traveling to any place in the United States, *tape your pet's health certificate (stating rabies vaccination date and type) onto the kennel.* Some states have become quite formidable. Georgia recently impounded somebody's pet that arrived without its documents and slapped it into quarantine for *120 days* at $5 a day. Let it not happen to you!

Airlines will not check your pet through if you're making connecting flights. You must reclaim and recheck your animal at each transfer point, so bear this in mind when you're making out your schedule.

Fortunately, domestic air travel is *not* expensive for your pet. Most airlines charge you *200% of the excess-baggage rate* for your one-way jet coach fare. Sometimes they refer to it as the *extra-piece rate*, but what they mean is:

If your ticket costs from

$.00 to $25 your pet will cost	$8
$25.01 to $50	$10
$50.01 to $120	$12
$120.01 to $200	$14
$200.01 and over	$16

Thus, if it costs you $75 one way to fly from New York to Miami, it will cost you $12 for your animal, regardless of its size and weight or its kennel's size and weight.

Some airlines require that animals exceeding a certain size must travel as air freight. If you're shipping your animal by itself, it will *always* go air freight. They will weigh your pet and its kennel. That combined weight will then be multiplied by 165% of the normal air-freight rate for the route involved. Just hypothetically speaking, suppose the air-freight from New York to Philadelphia is 10 cents a pound. The rate for your pet is then 17 cents a pound (10 cents multiplied by 1.65 = 16.50 cents, then rounded to 17 cents). There is usually a minimum charge, i.e., you'll be charged for 50 pounds even if your pet plus its kennel weighs only 35 pounds. So ask about this whenever you're sending an animal as cargo.

AIR NEW ENGLAND

Cabin: Except for Seeing Eye dogs, pets must travel in baggage compartment.

Kennels: No, you must provide your own.

Reservations: It's important to notify them when you make your reservation that your pet will accompany you. They fly small aircraft with limited baggage space. If there's no room for your pet, they'll ship it after you on the first available flight.

Shipping Costs: This is one airline that will include your pet in your excess-baggage allowance. They levy a $2 minimum charge and if your pet plus your luggage total to 40 pounds or less, that's all you pay. If they add up to more than 40 pounds, you pay 10 cents for each additional pound.

Air Freight: They do not guarantee that your pet will be on the same plane as yourself. The cost depends on the air-freight rate for your destination multiplied by the weight of your pet plus its kennel. For example, between New York and Hyannis, a dog weighing less than 100 pounds costs $10 and a dog weighing more than 100 pounds costs $14.

Insurance: Not available.

AIR WEST

Cabin: No, except for Seeing Eye dog accompanying passenger.

Kennels: Yes, they have 3 sizes for sale. Prices do not include tax.

L x W x H	Cost	Accommodates
19" x 12" x 15"	$11	Toy breeds
22" x 17" x 17"	$14	Small dogs
40" x 20" x 27"	$28	Large dogs, and can be shipped on DC 9's only

Shipping Costs: Your pet will travel at 200% of the excess-baggage rate based on your normal one-way fare. See page 72 for explanation.

Shipping Procedure: Small and medium-sized pets normally travel in the front of the airliner, right behind the captain. Large pets will have to travel in the baggage compartment of the first available DC 9. Be sure to notify them when you make your flight reservation that your pet is traveling too, and tell them its size.

Insurance: Air West assumes no liability for your pet.

ALASKA AIRLINES

Cabin: No, except Seeing Eye dogs.
Kennels: Yes, they have wooden kennels available as follows:

Type	L x W x H	Cost
Small	20" x 14" x 16"	$9.50
Medium	25" x 18" x 19"	$12.25
Large	36" x 22" x 28"	$16.75
Extra-large	42" x 25" x 30"	$21.50

Shipping Costs: Your pet accompanying you on the same flight travels for 200% of the excess-baggage rate, which depends on your fare (see page 72 for a complete explanation). If it is shipped alone, your pet travels as air freight at 165% of the normal air-freight rate for the route involved (see pages 72–73 for explanation).

Shipping Procedure: To insure both space and a kennel for your pet, notify the airline that it will be traveling when you make your own reservation—a few days in advance. On the day of the flight, take your pet to the airport check-in counter a half hour or so before the recommended time.

When your pet is traveling as air freight, take it and its kennel to the cargo office at least 2 hours before your plane is scheduled to leave. It's also wise to call them a day in advance so they'll be prepared to handle the animal.

Insurance: Alaska Airlines accepts no liability for pets, so you'll have to insure independently.

ALLEGHENY AIRLINES

Cabin: Seeing Eye dogs only.

Kennels: They have wooden kennels available in 4 sizes:

Number	L x W x H	Cost	Accommodates
0	22" x 12" x 15"	$10	Miniature dogs
1	25" x 18" x 19"	$11	Beagles, etc.
2	36" x 22" x 26"	$16	Boxers, etc.
3	42" x 25" x 29½"	$18	Collies, setters, etc.

Shipping Costs: Animals that fit kennels 0 and 1 may travel at 200% of the excess-baggage rate for your one-way fare (see page 72 for explanation).

Animals that fit kennels 2 and 3 must be sent as air freight at 180% of the normal air-freight rate for your destination. For example, if you're traveling between New York and Pittsburgh, your pet plus its kennel will cost you 22 cents a pound, or approximately $10 if their combined weight is under 100 pounds.

Shipping Procedure: Alert the airline when you make your reservation, preferably a day or so in advance, that your pet will be traveling and discuss which size kennel they should have available. If you're making connections, *your pet must be reclaimed and rechecked at each transfer point.* Be sure to allow enough time for this. *Attach your pet's health certificate to its kennel.*

Check-in: They recommend that you check in a half hour early if your pet is traveling as excess baggage and 2 or more hours early if it's being sent as air freight.

Insurance: You are allowed to take out excess-valuation insurance on your pet and you purchase this at the ticket counter. Costs for this insurance were not available.

AMERICAN AIRLINES

Cabin: Yes, they permit small household pets (two to a cabin) that can fit a kennel measuring no more than 45″ (length + width + height). They provide this size carrier free of charge at the check-in counter but it's wise to request one in advance when you make your reservation.

Kennels: Yes, there are 3 sizes of plastic kennels available for larger pets. Prices quoted do not include tax.

Number	L x W x H	Cost	Accommodates
1	22″ x 12″ x 15″	$14	Small dogs, cats
2	26″ x 18″ x 19″	$17	Medium-sized dogs
3	36″ x 22″ x 26″	$26	Large dogs up to 70 pounds

You must provide your own kennels for animals weighing more than 70 pounds.

Shipping Costs: Animals weighing up to 115 pounds may travel at 200% of the normal excess-baggage rate for your one-way ticket (see page 72 for explanation). On a New York to Los Angeles flight, your pet would cost $14. Animals weighing more than 115 pounds must be shipped air freight at 165% of normal air-freight rates for your destination multiplied by the combined weight of your pet and its kennel. For a New York to California flight, you'd be charged a minimum of $39.90, which includes up to 50 pounds. Between 50 and

100 pounds, you'd pay 76 cents a pound additional or the 100-pound rate of $54.14, whichever is cheaper.

Shipping Procedure: They prefer to be notified about your pet when you make your seat reservation, and they are confident that you could arrive at normal check-in time and all would be well when your pet is traveling as excess baggage. We remain cautious, however, and advise you get there a half hour earlier.

The air-freight people would prefer that you arrive with your pet 2 hours before the normal check-in time.

Insurance: American Airlines assumes liability up to $500, and you may purchase additional insurance up to $2,500. Rates per $100 excess valuation were unavailable, but they will probably be either 10 or 20 cents per $100.

International Flights: The excess-baggage rates are figured in the same way as for domestic flights. But international rates apply for air freight and vary according to your destination.

BRANIFF INTERNATIONAL

Cabin: No, your pet will travel in the baggage compartment.

Kennels: Yes, 3 sizes of plywood kennels are on sale at the airport ticket counter. Prices quoted do not include tax.

L x W x H	Weight	Cost	Accommodates
24" x 17" x 18"	17 lbs.	$10	Cats, cocker spaniels, beagles, etc.
36" x 22" x 26"	33 lbs.	$15	Dalmatians, boxers, standard poodles, Springer spaniels, etc.
42" x 24" x 30"	41 lbs.	$20	Collies, Dobermans, setters, retrievers, etc.

Shipping Costs: If you are taking your pet with you, it travels at 200% of the normal one-way excess-baggage rate for your destination (see page 72 for explanation).

If you are shipping your pet alone, it travels as air freight at 165% of the regular cargo rate for your destination. For an animal plus kennel weighing 100 pounds or less, it would cost approximately $34 to fly from New York to Houston.

Shipping Procedure: Notify the airline at least 24 hours in advance that your pet will be traveling. The arrangements for it will be handled with your ordinary baggage at the airport check-in counter. If your pet is a dog, *you must bring along its rabies vaccination certificate.*

If you send your pet air freight, you should report to the cargo building with it 4 hours before flight time.

Insurance: You may purchase insurance for your pet at the rate of $1 per $100 excess valuation. Maximum valuation is set at $2,500.

CONTINENTAL AIRLINES

Cabin: Yes, if your pet is small and can fit under the seat. You needn't keep your animal in a case, but it should be leashed or under your control at all times. If it's in a case, the combined length, height and width of the case should add up to no more than 45″. You needn't be fancy, they said, a shoe box would do very well. No doubt it would, and it certainly gives you a vivid picture of what they mean by small.

Kennels: They have 5 sizes available, which makes them one of the best-equipped airlines around in this respect. Their kennels are made of wood and range as follows:

Number	L x W x H	Cost
1	12″ x 15″ x 18″	$10 plus tax
2	15½″ x 17″ x 24″	$12 ″ ″
3	19″ x 19″ x 26″	$14 ″ ″
4	22″ x 24″ x 35″	$17 ″ ″
5	24″ x 30″ x 40″	$23 ″ ″

Shipping Costs: When flying as excess baggage, your pet will cost 200% of your ticket's normal rate (see page 72 for a full explanation). Continental's economy fares are often lower than those offered by other airlines but this will not be reflected in your pet's traveling cost. For example, the usual one-way passenger fare for a Chicago to Colorado Springs flight is $71 for you and $12 for your pet. Continental's fare is $64 for you but remains $12 for your pet.

When flying as air freight, your pet will cost 165% of the normal air freight charged for your destination. For a Chicago to Colorado Springs flight, your pet will cost a minimum of $16, which includes up to 55 pounds. If your pet plus its kennel weighed 127 pounds, it would cost $31 or so for that same flight.

Shipping Procedure: Mention that you're taking your pet when you make your reservation and tell them what kennel size you'll need.

They recommend that you check in 45 minutes before flight time if your pet is traveling as excess baggage.

The air-freight people say that they can get your pet aboard your plane in good order if you arrive anywhere between 2 hours to 45 minutes before departure time when you're sending your pet as cargo.

Insurance: The first $50 liability is free. You can buy additional insurance for 10 cents per $100 additional valuation.

DELTA AIR LINES

Cabin: No, Seeing Eye dogs only.
Kennels: They sell 2 sizes at their airport ticket counters:

L x W x H	Cost	Accommodates
17″ x 18″ x 24″	$10	Animals measuring no more than 14″ at shoulder
22″ x 26″ x 36″	$15	Animals measuring no more than 22″ at shoulder

Shipping Costs: If your animal accompanies you, it will cost 200% of the normal excess-baggage rate (see page 72 for explanation).

Freight: If you ship your animal alone, it will travel as air freight at 165% of the normal air-freight rate for your destination multiplied by the combined weight of your pet and its kennel. For example, the charge on a New York to Atlanta flight would be about $32 for a dog and kennel weighing 100 pounds.

Shipping Procedure: Notify them in advance that your pet is coming along and tell them which kennel you'll need. Allow 15 to 30 minutes extra to check in. If you're sending your pet as air freight, take it to the cargo office 2½ to 3 hours before departure time.

Insurance: If you want insurance for your animal, purchase it at one of the independent insurance companies at the airport.

EASTERN AIRLINES

Cabin: No, Seeing Eye dogs only.

Kennels: Yes, they have 4 sizes for sale at most of the airports they serve. At smaller airports, they stock the most commonly used sizes. Guess who that leaves out? You can buy the kennel at any time prior to flight departure.

L x W x H	Cost
22″ x 12″ x 15″	$9.50
26″ x 18″ x 19″	$10.50
36″ x 22″ x 26″	$15.50
43″ x 25″ x 30″	$20.50

Shipping Costs: Pets accompanying the owner are carried at 200% of the normal excess-baggage rate (see page 72 for explanation).

Shipping Procedure: They like to be notified in advance that your pet will be traveling with you, preferably when you make your reservation. Your pet will be checked in with your luggage at the airport ticket counter. They can't guarantee that your pet will travel on the same plane as yourself, but the chances of your being separated are extremely remote.

Insurance: Eastern is liable up to $500 per ticket, which includes your pet. If you wish to declare additional valuation, you may at the rate of 10 cents per $100 above $500 up to a maximum of $5,000.

Internationally, the limit of liability depends on weight.

EXECUTIVE AIRLINES

Cabin: Yes, if under 10 pounds, and they prefer your pet to travel in a carrier.

Kennels: No, but at large airports they help you purchase one from another airline.

Shipping Costs: Your pet plus its kennel will cost 10 cents a pound, no matter whether you're flying from Boston to Nantucket or from Miami to Jacksonville.

Shipping Procedure: They advise you to arrive with your pet 1 hour before the normal check-in time.

They check your pet only from point to point, so if you're making a connecting flight you must reclaim and recheck your pet.

Insurance: Executive's limit of liability is $500 per person. If you wish to declare additional valuation on your pet, you will have to show some proof, such as AKC papers, in order to purchase additional coverage.

MOHAWK AIRLINES—See Allegheny Airlines

NATIONAL AIRLINES

Cabin: No, Seeing Eye dogs only.

Kennels: Yes. As this book was going to print, they were expecting new polystyrene models and you should check with them about this. The only information we have available is on the older-style plywood kennels:

L x W x H	Cost	Accommodates
25" x 16" x 18"	$10	Animals up to 20 lbs.
33" x 24" x 26"	$15	Animals up to 35 lbs.

Shipping Costs: Animals that fit in these kennels fly at 200% of the normal one-way excess-baggage rate (see page 72 for explanation).

Larger animals must fly as air freight at 165% of the normal air-freight rate multiplied by the combined weight of your pet plus its kennel. For example, the normal 50-pound minimum charge on a New York to Miami flight is $17.50. It will be $25.25 or thereabouts for your pet plus its kennel if they total to 50 pounds or less.

Shipping Procedure: Reserve space for your pet when you make your own reservations. They recommend you check in 45 minutes before the normally recommended time. You should arrive 2½ hours before departure time when you're sending your pet as air freight. Report to the airport ticket counter.

Insurance: Additional valuation may be declared and purchased at the rate of 10 cents per $100 additional up to a maximum of $2,500.

New York Airways Helicopter

It's a shame but our pets—not to mention ourselves—miss out on a lovely adventure. They don't accept *any* animals.

North Central Airlines

Cabin: No.

Kennels: Allow 48 hours prior to departure for them to locate the appropriate kennel for your animal, which clearly indicates they need advance notice that your pet will be traveling and information as to its size and weight. Their kennels are sterilized fiber glass and are listed as follows:

Cost	Accommodates
$10.50	Toy breeds
$12.50	Small dogs
$21.50	Medium dogs
$26.50	Large dogs

Shipping Costs: Your pet travels at 200% of your ticket's regular excess-baggage rate (see page 72 for explanation).

Shipping Procedure: Take your pet to the airport check-in counter 45 minutes before the recommended time. North Central will not check an animal beyond transfer points, so if you're making a connecting flight you'll have to allow time to reclaim and recheck your pet.

Insurance: No information available.

NORTHEAST AIRLINES

Cabin: No, if you're flying domestic. Yes, if you're flying to the Bahamas or Bermuda. In which case, your pet is allowed on board only if its carrier will fit under your seat.

Kennels: If you provide your own kennel it must not exceed 98″ (length plus width plus height). Northeast sells two sizes:

L x W x H	Cost
16″ x 19″ x 25″	$10
24″ x 27″ x 33″	$15

Shipping Costs: Domestically, your pet travels in the baggage compartment of your plane for 200% of the excess-baggage charge (see page 72 for explanation).

When your pet travels alone, it's sent as air freight and must be taken to the air-freight office. There is a minimum charge of $10. Air-freight rates vary according to the route involved.

Internationally, your pet will cost you 1% of the first-class fare for the route involved per kilo (2.2 pounds) for the combined weight of your pet and its kennel. If you send your pet on alone, you will be charged the appropriate air-freight rate based on the route traveled.

Shipping Procedure: Reserve space for your pet when you make your initial reservation. When your pet's coming along with you as excess baggage, just take it to the airport check-in counter a half hour earlier than the recommended predeparture time. When you're shipping your pet as air freight, you must take it to the cargo office approximately 4 hours before departure. If Northeast is unable to place your animal on the same flight you're taking, which rarely happens, they'll warn you in advance.

Insurance: Northeast accepts no liability for your animal. Should you wish to insure it, you'll have to purchase insurance at one of the independent companies at the airport terminal.

Northwest Orient Airlines

Cabin: Yes, a small household pet in a kennel not exceeding 8″ high can travel in the cabin with you. You must be sure to tranquilize the animal *and* keep it in its carrier.

Kennels: No, you will have to provide your own.

Shipping Costs: Whether your animal travels with you in the cabin or is placed in the baggage compartment, the cost of its ticket will be 200% of your normal one-way excess-baggage rate (see page 72 for explanation).

If your animal requires a kennel larger than 98″ (add the height, length and width of the kennel) it must travel as air freight. You'll be charged 165% of the normal air-freight rate multiplied by the combined weight of your animal and its kennel. If you're shipping your animal by itself, it will travel as air freight.

Shipping Procedure: Reserve space for your animal when you make your own reservation. When your animal will be traveling as air freight, call the cargo department at least a day in advance of your flight to be sure they are expecting it.

The travel arrangements for an animal going as excess baggage are handled at the airport check-in counter. You'll need at least 15 minutes more than the suggested check-in time. When your pet is flying as air freight, take it at least 2 hours in advance of flight time to the air-freight office.

In addition, be sure to have your pet's health certificate, including rabies vaccination information, taped to its kennel. Northwest reminds you that *cats* too need rabies vaccination to enter several states. Please check pages 44–61 for your destination state's entry requirements.

Insurance: Yes, you may purchase additional valuation for your pet, but rate information was unavailable.

International Flights: Kennel availability is the same. For rate differences check with the airline.

OZARK AIRLINES

Cabin: No, Seeing Eye dogs only.

Kennels: Yes, they have 4 sizes in polyethylene kennels. Order a kennel when you make your reservations.

Number	L x W x H	Cost	Dom. Vol. Wt.	Accommodates
#0	19" x 12" x 15"	$12.75	22 lbs.	Toy dogs, all cats, Chihuahuas, Yorkshire terriers
#1	22" x 17" x 17"	$14.75	38 lbs.	Beagles, cockers, fox terriers, miniature poodles
#2	31" x 19" x 22"	$24.75	75 lbs.	Boxers, Dalmatians, Springer spaniels, standard poodles
#3	38" x 20" x 26"	$29.75	106 lbs.	Collies, retrievers, setters, shepherds

Shipping Costs: Your pet travels for 200% of the excess-baggage rate based on your one-way jet-coach fare, the price ranging from $8 to $16 (see page 72 for a full explanation).

When you ship an animal by itself, it will cost 165% of the air-freight rate normally charged for the destination involved. The combined weight of your animal and its kennel will then be multiplied by the air-freight rate.

Shipping Procedure: As mentioned earlier, you reserve space for your pet when you make reservations and tell them which kennel size to have available. On the day of departure, report to the airport check-in counter at least a half hour earlier than the recommended time.

When you ship your animal as air freight, call that office a day in advance and make definite delivery and kennel arrangements with them. Take your pet to them 2 to 4 hours ahead of departure time.

PAN AMERICAN AIRWAYS—See page 184.

PIEDMONT AIRLINES

Cabin: Yes, a small household pet in an appropriate kennel, which can fit under the seat, is allowed. Seeing Eye dogs accompanying a passenger are also permitted.

Kennels: Four sizes of polyethylene plastic kennels are sold at the airport check-in counter. Prices quoted do not reflect local sales taxes.

Type	*L x W x H*	*Cost*
Toy	19″ x 12″ x 15″	$12
Small	22″ x 17″ x 17″	$14
Medium	31″ x 19″ x 22″	$23
Large	38″ x 20″ x 26″	$28

Shipping Costs: Your pet travels for 200% of the excess-baggage rate based on your one-way jet-coach fare. It will cost from $8 to $16 (see page 72 for a full explanation).

When you ship a pet by itself, you'll be charged for the combined weight of your animal plus its kennel multiplied by 165% of the normal air-freight rate for the route involved.

Shipping Procedure: Reserve a kennel for your pet when you make your own reservation. Be sure to have your animal's health certificate taped to its kennel. Arrive 1 hour in advance of the normal check-in time on the day of departure. Report to the airport check-in counter.

If you're making connecting flights, allow enough time to reclaim and recheck your animal.

When you send your pet air freight, take it to that office 2 to 3 hours in advance of departure time. It's a good idea to call the cargo people a day ahead.

Insurance: You can insure your animal when you're sending it air freight.

PILGRIM AIRLINES

Cabin: Yes, if it's a small animal in a case, and the plane is not crowded and no other passengers object. Pilgrim carries only 19 passengers per trip, so call in advance to reserve space on an uncrowded flight. They don't want you to be unhappy, however, and if they can manage to allow your pet to travel in the cabin with you, they will.

Kennels: No, you'll have to purchase one elsewhere.

Shipping Costs: $10 plus tax.

Shipping Procedure: It's to your own benefit to call them in advance about your pet. Let them know how large an animal it is to be sure they can accommodate it aboard their aircraft.

SOUTHERN AIRWAYS

Cabin: No, except for properly harnessed Seeing Eye dogs accompanying their owner.

Kennels: Yes, 3 sizes of polyethylene plastic kennels are sold at the airport check-in counter.

Make sure your pet has a place to stay.

Number	L x W x H	Cost	Accommodates
#0	19" x 12" x 15"	$11	Animals weighing 10–15 lbs.
#1	22" x 17" x 17"	$13	Animals weighing 30–35 lbs.
#2	32" x 20" x 25"	$22	Animals weighing 60–65 lbs.

Shipping Costs: Your pet travels for 200% of the excess-baggage rate based on your one-way jet-coach fare. It will cost from $8 to $16 (see page 72 for a full explanation).

Any animal requiring a size #2 kennel or being shipped by itself must travel as air freight. That will cost 165% of the normal air-freight rate for the route involved. The charge is figured by multiplying the combined weight of your animal plus its kennel by the appropriate rate.

Shipping Procedure: Reserve a kennel for your pet when you make your own reservation. If you're making connecting flights, allow enough time to reclaim and recheck your pet at transfer points. Take your pet to the airline check-in counter a half hour earlier than the normally recommended time. Be sure your pet's health documents are taped to its kennel.

Insurance: No information available.

Suburban Airlines

Cabin: No, except for Seeing Eye dogs.
Kennels: No, you'll have to provide your own.
Shipping Costs: There is a minimum charge of $5. They usually accept only small animals in a sturdy container, and $5 is the normal charge for their transportation. Somewhat larger pets would cost an additional 10 cents a pound for the combined weight of the animal plus its kennel. Information on the minimum weight base was unavailable.

Shipping Procedure: Give them advance notice that you're taking your pet and check in a half hour earlier than usually recommended. All arrangements will be handled at the airport check-in counter.

Insurance: No.

TWA—Trans World Airlines

Cabin: Hurray for TWA! They *will* allow you to take your pet into the cabin with you if it's a small or toy dog or a cat. Advise them in advance that your pet is coming along and they will furnish a collapsible kennel for $1.98. They also do their utmost to see that the seat next to you is vacant, which gives you more room and avoids annoying other passengers.

Kennels: They have a supply of polyethylene kennels available at all their major airports for pets traveling in the cargo compartment.

Type	Cost
Toy	$12.95
Small	$14.95
Medium	$24.95
Large	$29.95

Shipping Costs: Any pet accompanying the passenger, either in the cabin or in the cargo compartment, will cost $8 to $16. You'll be charged 200% of the normal excess-baggage rate based on your one-way jet-coach fare (see page 72 for a full explanation).

Shipping Procedure: Reserve a kennel for your pet when you make your own reservation, at least a day, preferably more, in advance. All the travel arrangements for your animal will be handled at the airport check-in counter. It's best to arrive 30 to 45 minutes in advance of the normal check-in time.

Insurance: No.

United Air Lines

Cabin: United deserves *three* rousing cheers; they just recently decided to permit small dogs, cats and household birds to accompany passengers in the cabin. The animal must be in a case measuring no more than 21″ long, 16″ wide and 8″ high, and it must be placed at your feet or under the seat in front of you. There's a limit of 1 kennel per cabin, so make your reservation early.

Kennels: Yes, they have 4 sizes available for sale at all their major airports. But they do appreciate being notified in advance which size you'll need.

Type	L x W x H	Weight	Cost
Small	16" x 14" x 20"	12 lbs.	$11
Medium	19" x 18" x 25"	18 lbs.	$12
Large	28" x 22" x 36"	37 lbs.	$17
Extra-large	35" x 22" x 36"	38 lbs.	$21

Shipping Costs: All animals, regardless of where they are carried, will cost $8 to $16, depending on your one-way jet-coach fare. You are charged 200% of the excess-baggage rate for your destination (see page 72 for a full explanation).

When you ship your animal by itself, you'll be charged 165% of the normal air-freight rate for the route involved multiplied by the weight of your animal plus its kennel.

Shipping Procedure: As you can see, it's necessary to let them know you'll be taking your pet when you make your own reservation. If you want to keep your pet in the cabin, reserve as far in advance as possible. Otherwise, give them at least 1 day's notice.

Take your pet to the airport check-in counter at least a half hour in advance of the recommended time.

If you're shipping your animal air freight, take it to the cargo building 2 hours before your scheduled departure time.

Insurance: All animals are automatically insured for $500 if they're accompanying you on the same flight. When you ship an animal, or if you wish to buy additional insurance for your pet, you buy that insurance at the air-freight office for 20 cents per $100 up to a maximum of $10,000.

WESTERN AIRLINES

Cabin: No, Seeing Eye dogs only.

Kennels: Yes, they have 3 sizes available:

L x W x H	Cost	Accommodates
19″ x 19″ x 26″	$14	Terriers, etc.
22″ x 24″ x 35″	$17	Water spaniels, etc.
24″ x 30″ x 40″	$22	Collies, German shepherds, etc.

Shipping Costs: If your pet accompanies you on the same flight (which they assure you it will), it will cost between $8 and $16, depending on your one-way jet-coach fare. This charge is computed at 200% of the normal excess-baggage rate for your destination (see page 72 for a full explanation).

An animal traveling by itself will be sent as air freight, computed on the combined weight of the animal plus its kennel multiplied by 165% of the normal air-freight rate for the route involved.

Shipping Procedure: Notify them when you make your seat reservation that you're taking your pet and also tell them which size kennel you'll need, unless you have your own. Arrive at the ticket counter an hour before the recommended check-in time on the day of departure.

When you're shipping your animal, contact the air-freight office at least a day in advance of the flight. They would like you to bring your animal to them at least 2 hours before flight time.

Insurance: No, you'll have to purchase it independently.

WHAT TO DO
ALONG THE WAY

This section should reassure you that there is no lack of recreational facilities or accommodations for you while traveling around the United States with your pet. The private facilities available are simply too extensive to list so we have confined ourselves to national and state parks and major hotel and motel chains. We hope that these provide you with a general and encouraging picture.

NATIONAL PARKS

Our national parks are a delight to visit, wonderful for camping *and* they permit pets! We thought you'd like to know that you have hundreds of alternatives to hotels, motels and highway restaurants. So, if you'd like to camp out for a change, or simply stop to picnic in some of this country's most splendid scenery, you and your pet are welcome at all but four of the parks.

They do require you to keep your pet on a leash or otherwise physically restrained, and it will be excluded from food stores, public eating places, designated swimming beaches, park trails beyond a quarter of a mile from developed areas

Arrange for some side trips for your pet.

and park lands beyond the developed areas. But you'd probably not choose to let your pet go roaming at will, anyway, in a nature preserve where it's likely to bump into wild animals.

Most parks have an entrance fee that you can pay per day or you can buy a Golden Eagle Passport for $10, which is good for the entire calendar year in all Federal Recreation Fee Areas.

"Camping in the National Park System" costs only 25 cents and offers very complete information on each park. To get it, write to the Superintendent of Documents, U.S. Government Printing Office, Washington, D.C. 20402.

In the Stehekin Valley Campgrounds, a subdivision of North Cascades National Park Group, Sedro Woolley, Washington 98284, the following 4 campgrounds exclude pets (which still leaves you 6 others to choose from):

Bridge Creek Campgrounds
Cottonwood Campgrounds
Dolly Varden Campgrounds
Shady Campgrounds

The national parks that do accept pets are:

ALASKA

Glacier Bay National Monument
Box 1089
Juneau, Alaska 99801
Wilderness camping (throughout area)
Mount McKinley National Park
McKinley Park, Alaska 99755

ARIZONA

Canyon de Chelly National Monument
Box 588
Chinle, Ariz. 86503

Chiricahua National Monument
Dos Cabezas Star Route
Willcox, Ariz. 85643

Glen Canyon National Recreation Area
Box 1507
Page, Ariz. 86040

Grand Canyon National Park
Box 129
Grand Canyon, Ariz. 86023

Navajo National Monument
Tonalea, Ariz. 86044

Organ Pipe Cactus National Monument
Box 38
Ajo, Ariz. 85321

ARKANSAS

Hot Springs National Park
Box 1219
Hot Springs National Park, Ark. 71901

CALIFORNIA

Channel Islands National Monument
Box 1388
Oxnard, Calif. 93030

Death Valley National Monument
Death Valley, Calif. 92328

Devils Postpile National Monument
c/o Yosemite National Park
Box 577 (Yosemite Village)
Yosemite National Park, Calif. 95389

Joshua Tree National Monument
Box 875
Twentynine Palms, Calif. 92277

Kings Canyon National Park
Three Rivers, Calif. 93271

Lassen Volcanic National Park
Mineral, Calif. 96063

Lava Beds National Monument
Box 867
Tulelake, Calif. 96134

Pinnacles National Monument
Paicines, Calif. 95043

Point Reyes National Seashore
Point Reyes, Calif. 94956

Sequoia National Park
Three Rivers, Calif. 93271

Whiskeytown National Recreation Area
Box 188
Whiskeytown, Calif. 96095

Yosemite National Park
Box 577 (Yosemite Village)
Yosemite National Park, Calif. 95389

COLORADO

Black Canyon of the Gunnison National Monument
c/o Curecanti Recreation Area
334 S. 10th St.
Montrose, Colo. 81401

Colorado National Monument
c/o Curecanti Recreation Area
334 S. 10th St.
Montrose, Colo. 81401

Dinosaur National Monument
Box 101
Dinosaur, Colo. 81610

Great Sand Dunes National Monument
Box 60
Alamosa, Colo. 81101

Hovenweep National Monument
c/o Mesa Verde National Park
Mesa Verde National Park, Colo. 81330

Mesa Verde National Park
Mesa Verde National Park, Colo. 81330

Rocky Mountain National Park
Estes Park, Colo. 80517

Shadow Mountain Recreation Area
c/o Rocky Mountain National Park
Estes Park, Colo. 80517

FLORIDA

Everglades National Park
Box 279
Homestead, Fla. 33030

IDAHO

Craters of the Moon National Monument
Box 29
Arco, Idaho 83213

KENTUCKY

Cumberland Gap National Historical Park
Box 840
Middlesboro, Ky. 40965

Mammoth Cave National Park
Mammoth Cave, Ky. 42259

MAINE

Acadia National Park
Box 338
Bar Harbor, Maine 04609

MARYLAND

Assateague Island National Seashore
Route 2, Box 111
Berlin, Md. 21811

Catoctin Mountain Park
Thurmont, Md. 21788

Chesapeake and Ohio Canal National Monument
Box 158
Sharpsburg, Md. 21782

Greenbelt Park
6501 Greenbelt Road
Greenbelt, Md. 20770

MASSACHUSETTS

Cape Cod National Seashore
South Wellfleet, Mass. 02663

MICHIGAN

Isle Royale National Park
87 N. Ripley St.
Houghton, Mich. 49931

MISSISSIPPI

Natchez Trace Parkway
R.R. 5, NT-143
Tupelo, Miss. 38801

MISSOURI

Ozark National Scenic Riverways
Box 448
Van Buren, Mo. 63965

MONTANA

Bighorn Canyon National Recreation Area
Box 458 YRS
Hardin, Mont. 59035
Glacier National Park
West Glacier, Mont. 59936

NEVADA

Lake Mead National Recreation Area
601 Nevada Hwy.
Boulder City, Nev. 89005

NEW MEXICO

Bandelier National Monument
Los Alamos, N. Mex. 87544
Chaco Canyon National Monument
Star Route
Bloomfield, N. Mex. 87413

NEW YORK

Fire Island National Seashore
P.O. Box 229
Patchogue, N.Y. 11772

NORTH CAROLINA

Cape Hatteras National Seashore
Box 457
Manteo, N.C. 27954

NORTH DAKOTA

Theodore Roosevelt National Memorial Park
Medora, N. Dak. 58645

See that your pet attends to his toilet
before taking that long trip.

OKLAHOMA

Arbuckle National Recreation Area
c/o Platt National Park
Box 201
Sulphur, Okla. 73086
Platt National Park
Box 201
Sulphur, Okla. 73086

OREGON

Crater Lake National Park
Box 7
Crater Lake, Ore. 97604

PENNSYLVANIA

Fort Necessity National Battlefield
Route 1, Box 311
Farmington, Pa. 15437

SOUTH DAKOTA

Badlands National Monument
Box 72
Interior, S. Dak. 57750
Wind Cave National Park
Hot Springs, S. Dak. 57747

TENNESSEE

Great Smoky Mountains National Park
Gatlinburg, Tenn. 37738

TEXAS

Big Bend National Park
Big Bend National Park, Texas 79834

Padre Island National Seashore
Box 8560
Corpus Christi, Texas 78412

UTAH

Arches National Monument
c/o Canyonlands National Park
Post Office Bldg.
Moab, Utah 84532

Bryce Canyon National Park
Bryce Canyon, Utah 84717

Canyonlands National Park
Post Office Bldg.
Moab, Utah 84532

Capitol Reef National Monument
Torrey, Utah 84775

Natural Bridges National Monument
c/o Canyonlands National Park
Post Office Bldg.
Moab, Utah 84532

Zion National Park
Springdale, Utah 84767

VIRGINIA

Blue Ridge National Parkway
Box 1710
Roanoke, Va. 24008

Prince William Forest Park
Triangle, Va. 22172

Shenandoah National Park
Luray, Va. 22835

WASHINGTON

Coulee Dam National Recreation Area
Box 37
Coulee Dam, Wash. 99116

Mount Rainier National Park
Longmire, Wash. 98397

North Cascades National Park Group
Sedro Woolley, Wash. 98284

Olympic National Park
600 E. Park Ave.
Port Angeles, Wash. 98362

WYOMING

Devils Tower National Monument
Devils Tower, Wyo. 82714

Grand Teton National Park
Box 67
Moose, Wyo. 83012

Yellowstone National Park
Yellowstone National Park, Wyo. 83020

STATE PARKS

There are hundreds of state parks in this country and they *do* vary in their attitudes toward pets, ranging from severe Pennsylvania to lenient Utah. We've included each state's park regulations to help you avoid the annoyance of detouring to get to a park only to find it closed to your pet. If you know the regulations in advance, you can plan your picnics and choose your campsites where you know both you and your pet will be welcomed.

ALABAMA

You are allowed to bring a dog or other animal into Alabama state parks provided it is kept under your immediate control at all times. Dogs must be restrained on a leash not longer than 6'. The following parks *do not* permit pets.

Cheaha, near Talladega
Gulf, near Gulf Shores
Little Mountain, near Guntersville

ALASKA

As yet, Alaska has no state parks. There are, however, a great many state waysides at which you can camp and picnic in the company of your pet, provided it's on a leash. For a list of these waysides and other tourist information, write Alaska Travel Division, Pouch E, Juneau, Alaska 99801.

ARIZONA

The only restriction mentioned for Arizona state parks is that you keep your pet on a leash.

ARKANSAS

Campers and visitors to Arkansas state parks may bring their dogs, leashed, but dogs are not permitted to run at large or create disturbances that would annoy other people. The State Parks, Recreation and Travel Commission at 149 State Capitol, Little Rock, Arkansas 72201 will send you additional tourist information.

CALIFORNIA

You'll have to pay a 50-cent charge for each pet in California parks. They allow you to bring your pet along, provided it's on a leash no longer than 6'. At night you must keep your pet in a tent or in an enclosed vehicle.

P.S. These rules apply to California state beaches as well.

Colorado

The only information available on Colorado state parks' regulations for pets stated that you must keep your animal on a leash.

Connecticut

Pets are permitted if they're on a leash and under their owners' control. They are not allowed in Connecticut state campgrounds from May 1 to September 30. From October 1 through April 30, pets are allowed but there must be no more than one per campsite and that pet must be on a leash no longer than 6'.

The following are the only Connecticut state parks that do *not* permit pets at all:

> Sherwood Island, near Westport
> Squantz Pond, near New Fairfield

Delaware

As far as we could discover, pets are permitted on leashes in the facilities listed below, but we can't give a blanket ruling on other Delaware state parks:

> Cape Henlopen, near Lewes, on State 18
> Delaware Seashore, near Rehoboth Beach, on State 14
> Trap Pond, near Laurel, off State 24

Florida

You must keep your pet on a leash at all times in Florida state parks and historic memorials. It's strictly picnicking for you in these facilities because pets are never allowed in camping or swimming areas nor may they remain anywhere in the parks overnight.

GEORGIA

Georgia state parks allow dogs only and they must be kept on a leash at all times. Also, they are excluded from swimming areas, cottages, mobile homes and park buildings.

HAWAII

Pets are allowed in Hawaii state parks but they're not permitted to run at large in park grounds or buildings.

IDAHO

Pets are permitted in all Idaho state parks if they're on a leash.

ILLINOIS

Pets are permitted if they are leashed in all Illinois state parks except the ones listed below:

> Douglas County, near Oakland
> Illinois Beach, near Waukegan
> Pyramid, at Pinckneyville

INDIANA

Pets on a 6′ leash are permitted in all Indiana state parks.

IOWA

Leashed pets are allowed in all Iowa state parks.

KANSAS

Pets are allowed if they're kept on a leash. However, you can't take your animal on any of the bathing beaches.

KENTUCKY

Kentucky state parks welcome pets if they're on a leash. But under no circumstances should you leave your animal alone in any of the lodge rooms or cottages.

LOUISIANA

The only requirement listed is that pets be kept on a leash.

MAINE

Except for the parks listed below, pets are allowed in all Maine state parks if they're kept on a leash:

Baxter, near Millinocket

Sebago Lake, near Naples

MARYLAND

Sorry, pets are not allowed in Maryland state parks, with two exceptions:

Elk Neck, near North East, on Route 272. Pets permitted in camping area

Milburn Landing, near Pocomoke City, off Route 364. In camping areas only

Should you want to camp or picnic in the state forests, however, you are allowed to bring your pet. The only exception is Seth Forest, which is strictly for research purposes.

To write for camping information (or to register a protest): Maryland Department of Forest and Parks, State Office Building, Annapolis, Maryland 21404.

MASSACHUSETTS

Your pet must be appropriately restrained—leash, bridle, tether or cage. No pet is permitted in bathing areas in the state parks.

MICHIGAN

Pets are permitted in all Michigan state parks if they are kept on a leash not exceeding 6'. Animals are not allowed in bathing areas.

MINNESOTA

Here again, pets are allowed if on a leash. However, they are excluded from all state park buildings.

MISSISSIPPI

Pets are allowed in all state parks if they're on a leash.

MISSOURI

Pets are allowed in all state parks if they're leashed.

MONTANA

You are required to keep your pet on a leash in Montana state parks and campgrounds from April 1 through September 15 each year, when the parks are most heavily visited.

NEBRASKA

Your dog must be kept on a leash in Nebraska state parks and recreation areas. Cats and other household-type pets must be appropriately restrained.

NEVADA

The only requirement stated is that you keep your animal on a leash.

NEW HAMPSHIRE

Pets, if they're leashed, are allowed in all state parks but they're not permitted on the beach or in the water.

NEW JERSEY

The only information available stated that you must keep your animal leashed.

New Mexico

The most that's required of your animal is that it be on a leash in some New Mexico state parks; pets are permitted in all.

New York

To our great delight New York just liberalized its rulings on pets and most state parks now allow them in the camping areas. Dogs must be leashed, however, and you must bring along the rabies vaccination certificate. The following parks *do not permit* pets at all:

> Clarence Fahnestock Memorial, near Carmel
> Darien Lakes, near Darien Center
> Hamlin Beach, near Hamlin
> Hither Hills, near Montauk
> Lake Taghkanic, near Hudson
> Lakeside Beach, near Kuckville
> Letchworth, near Perry
> Margaret Lewis Norrie, near Hyde Park
> Wildwood, near Wading River

These allow *dogs* only:

> Bowman Lake, near Oxford
> Chenango Valley, near Binghamton
> Delta Lake, near Rome
> Gilbert Lake, near Oneonta
> Green Lakes, near Fayetteville
> John Boyd Thacher, near East Berne
> Moreau Lake, near Glens Falls
> Pixley Falls, near Boonville
> Selkirk Shores, near Pulaski

North Carolina

Only dogs are permitted in North Carolina state parks, and they must be kept on a leash not exceeding 6′. They are also excluded from swimming areas, cabins and cabin areas.

North Dakota

Be sure to bring your dog's health certificate stating it has been inoculated against rabies at least 30 days in advance of entering North Dakota. The only other requirement is that you keep your pet on a leash.

Ohio

Pets, if they're leashed or otherwise restrained, are allowed in state park picnic areas but they're not permitted in cabins, camping areas or bathing beaches.

Oklahoma

Pets, on a leash, are permitted in all Oklahoma state parks.

Oregon

Pets are welcome in Oregon state parks but they must be on a leash or in a vehicle, tent, or otherwise controlled and confined. Pet owners are requested to keep their animals out of park buildings, prevent their pets from molesting wildlife, and see to it that they create no nuisance to other visitors.

Pennsylvania

Pets are not allowed in any Pennsylvania state park overnight accommodation or in any swimming area.

Rhode Island

When you visit Rhode Island state parks, just bring along your pet's health certificate and keep your pet on a leash.

South Carolina

Keep your pet on a leash in South Carolina state parks. You'll be asked to remove the animal if it causes a disturbance. Pets are not allowed in park cottages.

South Dakota

The only requirement is that you keep your pet on a leash.

Tennessee

Dogs, cats and other pets are permitted if on a leash or otherwise under some form of physically restrictive control. Except for Seeing Eye dogs, pets are not allowed in public eating places, food stores and on designated swimming beaches. Any animal harming either humans or wildlife will be either removed from the park or disposed of.

Texas

Their only requirement is that you keep your pet on a leash.

Utah

Pets are allowed in all Utah state parks if they're kept on a leash.

Vermont

You must have your animal's health certificate *and* keep your pet on a leash in any Vermont state park.

Virginia

The only restriction is that pets must be kept leashed.

Washington

Dogs and cats if on a leash are allowed in Washington state parks but they're not permitted on trails, in dining rooms, kitchens or swimming areas.

WEST VIRGINIA

Pets are permitted if leashed.

WISCONSIN

Pets are allowed if kept on a leash 8′ or shorter. They are not allowed on beaches or in public buildings.

WYOMING

There are no restrictions mentioned for Glendo State Park or Guernsey State Park. The remaining parks require that you keep your pet on a leash.

HOTELS AND MOTELS

Are you worried that if you bring your pet, you'll find no lodging for the night? Have no fear! You may arrive at any airport, drive along any highway or visit any city in the United States and be guaranteed a place for you both to stay.

Every major hotel and motel chain publishes a free brochure listing all the hotels under their management, with a description of the facilities available, the rates charged and, usually, a road map to illustrate hotel location vis-à-vis major highways. In addition to the chains, you will find an infinite number of privately owned hotels and motels that will accept you with your pet. The Automobile Association of America publishes directories of these private establishments, and their entries usually indicate whether or not animals are allowed. The *Mobil Travel Guide* series is another source of really thorough, reliable information on available accommodations. Each volume covers a major region of the United States and costs $3.95 at most bookstores.

In regard to the major chains, we list them here solely on

the basis of their policies toward pets—and for no other reason. We have nothing to say—good, bad or indifferent—about their facilities. If you, as a pet owner, have an opinion you'd like to share, we'd be very interested in hearing from you.

Holiday Inns, with very few exceptions, not only welcome pets but provide free kennels for their animal guests.

Howard Johnson's Motor Lodges accept pets, unless the individual entry states "No Pets" or "Small Pets Only."

The *Marriott* chain accepts pets other than the Great Dane variety in their ground-floor motel rooms, provided you sign a release accepting all responsibility for any damage your pet may cause. Their hotels accept lapdogs only.

Master Hosts Inns accept animals, unless prohibited by local ordinance, or the individual listing sports a square symbol indicating that that particular manager doesn't care for pets. Once again, you'll be held responsible for any damage caused by your pet.

Ramada Inns accept pets unless a listing specifically states otherwise. They also expect you to accept liability for any damage your pet may cause.

Sheraton Hotels and Motor Inns do not have a blanket policy in regard to animals. Only those entries which state "Pets" or "Small Pets" will accept your animal as a guest.

As always, the welcome extended to us depends on whether or not our pets are pleasant to have around. People's love for animals swiftly diminishes if they're kept awake at night by barking, or if they step out for a stroll and wind up in a mess. It's to our advantage, therefore, to make sure that our pets are considerate of the rights and paths of others.

FOREIGN
AFFAIRS

INSTEAD OF A PASSPORT

Good news . . . When you're making arrangements for foreign travel for your pet, you will be spared that wonderful moment when the passport photo is taken and the most graceful among us winds up looking like a drug addict who hasn't seen sunlight in 15 years. You will at least not have to look at such a picture of your animal friend. No photos and no passports or visas.

There are, however, documents that you *will* need for your pet. The specific requirements for papers and legalization procedures will be listed below for each country.

While procedures certainly vary from one country to another, we recommend that you have a certificate stating that your dog or cat has had a rabies shot and also a certificate stating that your pet has had (as recently as is possible) an examination by a vet and was found to be in good health. These papers should be sent to the federal veterinarian for your state for a legalizing stamp. (A list of these vets is found at the end of this chapter.) The federal vets usually are very prompt so that in just a few days you can have the basic papers for traveling.

Louie and I (Paula) have traveled around Europe a good deal. I was requested to show his papers only once—on our arrival in Amsterdam from New York. I always carried the

Let your pet enjoy the thrill of flight.

papers though, clipped into my own passport, and I checked on the requirements of each place we were to visit to make sure his papers were valid. As you will see, most of the documents require only a little effort to get and so it seems well worth while to have everything ready. To have to stop your trip or have your pet quarantined unnecessarily is a harassing, expensive experience. Put another way, it is fun to travel to new or foreign places with your pets. (Do remember that if you are traveling with feathered pets, check page 269 for re-entry requirements. It is helpful to get a permit from the Surgeon General covering psittacine birds *before* you leave.) A little attention and forethought make it possible to enjoy yourself and your pet. It's that simple. Have a good trip . . .

ENTRY REGULATIONS OF FOREIGN COUNTRIES

AFGHANISTAN

Proof of rabies inoculation and it's off to Kabul.

ALGERIA

Your pet will need a health certificate and proof of rabies shot. These should be sent to the federal vet for your state for certification. (A list of these vets will be found at the end of this chapter.)

ANGUILLA—See Caribbean Islands

ANTIGUA—See Caribbean Islands

ARGENTINA

When taking your dog or cat to Argentina, you will need a certificate stating that your pet has been inoculated with rabies vaccine and a statement that it is in good health. These documents will have to be certified by the federal vet in your state. (For a list of these vets by state, consult the end of this chapter.) It should take about a week for the documents to be returned to you, at which time they must be sent to the nearest Argentine Consulate for legalization. Their fee is about $8.50.

ARUBA—See Caribbean Islands

AUSTRALIA

If you are reading this book in New Zealand you will have no problem taking your dog or cat with you to Australia. At the time of writing, Australia will accept dogs or cats from no other country—with no exceptions. You can contact an Australian Consulate to see whether their policy has changed, but be advised that if it has, it will most likely have added importation from the United Kingdom only.

AUSTRIA

If you plan to travel in Austria for less than 6 months you need no special documents for taking your pet dog or cat. In fact, you are permitted to bring with you either 2 dogs or 2 cats. It is only required that the animals "should appear healthy," so take a good look before you go. If your pets are to be shipped to Austria and are not accompanied by you, you must apply for a permit. This permit is given by the Austrian Federal Ministry of Agriculture and you should contact your nearest Austrian Consulate for a copy. This same permit must be obtained if you are planning to take in animals other than dogs or cats.

BAHAMAS

If your dog or cat is less than 6 months old you will need a special permit from the

    Bahamas Ministry of Out Island Affairs
    Agriculture and Fisheries
    Nassau, Bahamas

Animals more than 6 months old must have a rabies vaccination administered *not less than 10 days or more than 9 months* before you leave for the islands. You will also have to go to a vet no sooner than *24 hours before departure* with your pet and have a health certificate made out.

BARBADOS—See Caribbean Islands

BELGIUM

You can of course apply to your nearest Belgian Consulate and get a four-page document that will give you all the details for the importation of your cat or dog. We will try to condense this information for you. Basically the procedure is that you take your pet to your vet and have him attest to the pet's good health and state the date of rabies vaccination and the type of vaccine that was used. This is an overview . . . the specifics follow. (You should be aware that once you have these documents you can arrive in the Netherlands, Luxembourg, the Netherlands Antilles and Surinam with no further documentation.)

The certificate filled out by the vet should include his name and address. He should then state the date on which your animal was vaccinated with anti-rabies vaccine. A brief description of the pet should follow, including its breed, age, color, markings and type of coat. It should also include your (the owner's) name and address. The vaccine must be one of the following kinds: A) inactivated nervous tissue base, or B) attenuated live "Flury" type. Then you need the manufacturing number, the name of the manufacturer, and the expiration date of the vaccine. (Gentle reader, don't despair . . . all of this is usually done as a matter of course whenever your pet is immunized, so you probably already possess such information.) Now make sure your vet has signed this information and then send it up to the federal veterinarian located in your state. (You will find their names and addresses listed at the end of this chapter.)

NOTE: Your dog or cat must have been vaccinated at least 30 days before you arrive in Belgium and the other countries mentioned above. If this hasn't been done the dog will probably be revaccinated at your place of arrival and it is likely that it will have to be quarantined (at your expense) for 30 days. So plan ahead. Now you may wonder how long this document is valid once you've gotten it made out and legalized by the federal vet. Well, it all depends! If your dog or cat was less than 3 months old when it got its shot, the certificate is valid for *6 months*. It is valid for *1 year* if the vaccine was either an inactivated type or Flury "HEP," and the pet was older than 3 months. If the dog or cat was older than 3 months when vaccinated with a Flury "LEP" shot, then the certificate is valid for *2 years*.

BERMUDA

At least *10 days before* you plan to leave for Bermuda, you must send to the

> Director of the Department of Agriculture and Fisheries
> Point Finger Road
> Paget, Bermuda

for a permit that will allow you to enter with your pet. Application forms for the permit can also be supplied by offices of the Bermuda government located in the large cities of the United States.

You will also need a rabies inoculation certificate attesting to the fact that the animal has been vaccinated *within 1 year of the time of departure*. The vet should also provide you with a certificate stating that the animal is free from disease and that the place where your pet has lived for the past 6 months has been rabies-free for a year.

BOLIVIA

Once you have had your dog or cat inoculated against rabies and can show proof of this you are prepared to travel to Bolivia.

BONAIRE—See Caribbean Islands

BOTSWANA

Your dog should have had a rabies vaccination *not more than 3 years or less than 30 days* prior to entry. For cats the inoculation should be *not less than 30 days or more than 1 year*. You will also have to get a health certificate from your vet. Then apply for an import permit, stating your name and address, the kind and number of animals you are bringing in and your destination in Botswana. For this you send to the

> Director of Veterinary Services
> Private Bag 3
> Gaberones, Botswana

BRAZIL

When you have a certificate stating that your pet has had its rabies shots, you can either take the certificate or mail it to the nearest Brazilian Consulate and they will stamp it. There is no charge for this stamp, but the document will be invalid without it.

BRITISH VIRGIN ISLANDS—See Caribbean Islands

BULGARIA

Your dog or cat must be vaccinated against rabies. Have your vet give you a statement attesting to this as well as a certificate of good health for your pet. These must be notarized.

BURMA

All you will need is a health certificate from a vet and proof that your dog or cat has had rabies shots.

CAMBODIA

You will need both a health certificate and a certificate stating that your pet has been inoculated with a rabies vaccine before you can enter Cambodia with either a dog or a cat.

CAMEROUN

Your pet must have had its rabies shot *more than 1 month but less than 6 months* before arrival.

CANADA

If you are going to Canada with your cat you can go on ahead without any special preparations. It will be looked at when you cross the border, but if it is not about to expire or isn't foaming at the mouth you shouldn't have any trouble. If you are going to Canada, or passing through Canada, from the United States with your dog you will need a certificate from a vet (licensed in either Canada or the U.S.) stating that your dog has received a rabies inoculation *within the past 12 months*. This certificate should also give a brief description of what the dog looks like.

NOTE: These regulations apply even if you're planning to be in Canada for just a few hours. So be prepared! If a dog is taken into Canada as part of some sort of entertainment or if it is a Seeing Eye dog you need no special documents.

CARIBBEAN ISLANDS

The following islands require certificates of rabies inoculation and certificates of good health issued by your vet:

Aruba
Bonaire
Curaçao
Guadeloupe
Martinique

Saba
St. Eustatius
St. Maarten

The islands below have quarantine periods of up to 6 months:

Anguilla	Grenada
Antigua	Nevis
Barbados	St. Kitts
British Virgin Islands	St. Lucia
Cayman Islands	St. Vincent
Dominique	

Information about the quarantine regulations is available from the Department of Agriculture and Fisheries for each island.

CAYMAN ISLANDS—See Caribbean Islands

CEYLON

You will need a health certificate from your vet stating that your pet is free from any contagious or infectious diseases. There is an import duty for animals which should amount to about $35 for dogs.

CHILE

When traveling to Chile with your pet you will need a health certificate from your vet. This certificate must then be sent to the federal veterinarian for your state. (The address of these officers will be found at the end of this chapter.) When you get the certificate back, it should be sent to the Chilean Consulate nearest you for legalization. They charge $9 for this service.

CHINA, PEOPLE'S REPUBLIC OF

Perhaps you might check The Little Red Book.

CHINA, REPUBLIC OF

Your dog or cat must be vaccinated with an anti-rabies serum and your vet should examine your pet and certify that it is in good health. You should, of course, have documents attesting to this when you and your pet arrive in the Republic of China. There is a *two-week quarantine* on arrival.

COLOMBIA

Any pet that you bring into Colombia must be accompanied by a health certificate made out by your vet. This must then be legalized by the Colombian Consulate nearest your home. The consular fee for this is $5.

COSTA RICA

Your dog or cat must be examined by your vet. He must give you a certificate stating that your pet is free from any contagious disease and that it has been vaccinated with an avianized rabies preparation. The shot must be administered *more than 1 month* but *less than 3 years* before entry. Bring a sample of your pet's stool when you bring the pet for this exam. It should be tested for Taenia Equinaococcus. (The health certificate should include the findings from this test.) Send the certificate to the federal vet for your state and request legalization. (A list of federal vets appears at the end of this chapter.) Send the legalized certificate to the Chief of the Veterinary Department, San Jose, Costa Rica, and request an entrance permit. If permission is granted, your pet may have to be quarantined for 6 months. They will let you know.

CURAÇAO—See Caribbean Islands

CYPRUS

There is *six-month* period of *quarantine* on Cyprus. If you are going to put your pet into quarantine, apply for a permit from the Chief Veterinary Officer on Cyprus for permission.

CZECHOSLOVAKIA

For both dogs and cats a health certificate will be required when entering Czechoslovakia. Your vet should include information that your pet is free from any infectious or contagious diseases.

DENMARK

Your pet dog or cat can be brought to Denmark as long as it is more than 4 months old. You should make sure that your pet has gotten its rabies shots *more than 4 weeks* and *less than 12 months* before it will enter Denmark. Your pet will be examined at the border by a veterinarian and will be given another rabies shot (unless you can prove that it got shots at a Danish border within the last 12 months.) Your pet will also be examined at the border. You must pay a small fee for this. Assuming that your pet is in good health and that you have papers showing that it has been vaccinated, you will be allowed into the country. There are 7 points at the border where you can have your pet examined. They are Elsinore, Copenhagen, Gedser, Rødby Ferry, Padborg and Krusaa, Frederikshavn, and Esbjerg.

NOTE: In order to make sure that a vet will be on hand when you are crossing into Denmark, you *must* write in advance. You should include in your letter a description of your pet, the point at which you will cross the border (remember, it must be one of the above 7) and the date you will arrive. Send this to

Veterinaerdirektortet
Nyropsgade, 37
DK 1602 Copenhagen V, Denmark

When you have received your answer, you are all set to travel to Denmark. Please keep in mind that these regulations stand and are enforced whether you are planning to arrive by plane, boat, car or train. These regulations are the same whether you are coming directly from the United States or from another point in Europe.

DOMINICAN REPUBLIC

To enter the Dominican Republic with your dog or cat you must have your vet make out a good-health certificate that you will have notarized. This then must be certified by your county clerk and then sent to the nearest consulate of the Dominican Republic for legalization. Their charge for legalization is $15.

DOMINIQUE—See Caribbean Islands

ECUADOR

Dogs and cats must be vaccinated with a rabies serum. The certificate attesting to this must be taken or sent to the consulate of Ecuador nearest you for a legalizing stamp. The consular fee for the legalization is $5.

EL SALVADOR

You will need a certificate stating that your dog or cat has had its rabies shots and you will also need a certificate from your vet stating that your pet is in good health. These certificates must then be taken or mailed to the nearest consulate of El Salvador, where they will be legalized. There is a consular charge of $10 for the two documents.

ENGLAND—See United Kingdom

FIJI

You cannot bring your pet to Fiji. If your plane or ship is making a stopover there your pet must not leave the transport.

Pets are allowed to change planes at Fiji if they don't dally—
no more than six hours is allowed for transit stops.

FINLAND

There is a *6-month quarantine* for dogs and cats. If you
still wish to import your pet, you must apply for a permit
from the

>   Ministry of Agriculture
>   Veterinary Department
>   Helsinki, Finland

You will need a health certificate and a rabies vaccination
certificate as well as proof of distemper shots. The rabies and
distemper shots should be given *not more than 3 weeks* prior
to entry.

Your pet will be examined upon arrival to make sure that
it is in good health. You must pay for the examination as well
as paying a fee for the importation and this will amount to
about $15. The cost of quarantine can be found out when
you apply for the import permit.

FRANCE

Have your vet make out a certificate stating that your dog
or cat has been inoculated with rabies vaccine that is "offi-
cially controlled" and make sure that this has been done *not
more than 6 months or less than 1 month* before you will enter France. *Bon voyage!*

GABON

Your dog and/or cat must have had rabies shots and an examination by a vet so that it can be declared in good health.
You must have the papers attesting to these facts and then
you both can take a trip to Gabon.

GERMANY, FEDERAL REPUBLIC OF

Taking your pet into Germany from the United States can be accomplished in one of two ways.

1. You can get a health certificate from your local vet. It should include your name and address and identify the breed, sex, age, type of coat, and markings of your pet. The certificate must also include the information that the pet has been inoculated with an approved rabies vaccine *not less than 30 days and not more than 12 months* before entering Germany.

2. If you don't have the time to have the pet inoculated and wait the 30 days, you can have the vet fill out the rest of the statement (see above) and include the information that:

(a) the animal was examined by him on such and such a day;

(b) the pet was found free of any suspicion of a contagious disease;

(c) and that for a period of at least 3 months there has been no case of rabies reported within a radius of 13 miles from where you live.

NOTE: Whichever form you choose, the vet must write on his official stationery and it must be *in German* or accompanied by an official German translation. The German Consulate will provide you with a sample copy of the certificate form in both English and German.

GHANA

Both dogs and cats will need to be vaccinated with an anti-rabies preparation, and you should have this certificate legalized by the federal veterinarian for your state. (For a listing of these vets consult the end of this chapter.) When you and your pet arrive in Ghana it will be examined by a vet to make sure that it is in good health.

GREAT BRITAIN—See United Kingdom

GREECE

Obtain a health certificate and certificate of rabies inoculation from your vet. This should then be sent to the federal vet for your state. (Addresses of the federal vets will be found at the end of this chapter.) This should take about a week. When you have the legalized certificate, it must be certified by the Greek Consulate for a fee of about $2.50.

GRENADA—See Caribbean Islands

GUADELOUPE—See Caribbean Islands

GUATEMALA

The tourist information sheet sent out by the government of Guatemala starts out with information about traveling with pets. In fact, they say, "We also want your pet to enjoy a Guatemalan vacation"—in our estimation, a most enjoyable attitude. You need to get a health certificate and some proof of vaccination against rabies. A Guatemalan Consulate will then legalize it *free of charge*. Happy vacation!

GUYANA

Your pet must have an anti-rabies vaccination and be given a clean bill of health by the vet. The vaccination must be given no less than *30 days* before departure. Then write for entry permission from:

Principal Veterinary Officer
Minister of Agriculture and Natural Resources
Brickdam, Georgetown
Guyana

When your pet arrives at Timehri Airport it will be checked out by a government vet. If this vet chooses, your animal may be quarantined at your expense. It would be a good idea, therefore, to request information about the standards for admission when you apply for entrance permission.

HAITI

Get your pet a rabies vaccination and good-health certificate from your vet and you're ready to go to Haiti.

HONDURAS, BRITISH

Once your vet has given you a certificate stating that your pet has received its rabies shots and is in good health, you must apply for entry permission from the Chief Agricultural Officer at Belmopan, British Honduras. Check at that time to make sure that your pet will not need to be quarantined. It will be examined on arrival.

HONDURAS, SPANISH

Your pet must have been vaccinated with a rabies serum and you must also have it examined by your vet so that it can have a certificate of good health. Both the health certificate and the rabies certificate should then be taken or mailed to a consulate of Honduras for legalization. There is no charge for this service.

HONG KONG

There is a *6-month quarantine* for dogs and cats coming from the United States. If you are planning to put your pet in quarantine you must first see that it has been examined by your vet and found to be healthy. This health certificate must accompany your pet when it arrives in Hong Kong. To apply for an import permit (which you will need in order to bring your pet into quarantine) write to:

Veterinary Regulatory Officer
Agriculture and Fisheries Department
393 Canton Road
Kowloon, Hong Kong.

Include in your application a description of your pet (its breed, age and sex) and also tell them when you expect to have your pet arrive. If it will be coming by plane, give the flight number and day of arrival; if by ship, the name of the ship and day of arrival.

HUNGARY

To bring your dog or cat into Hungary you must get a health certificate from your vet attesting to your pet's good health and stating that it has received inoculation against rabies. The certificate should also include your name and address and give a description of your dog. While cats do not need a rabies inoculation they should be accompanied by a health certificate.

ICELAND

Generally pets are not admitted to Iceland. Exceptions are made from time to time; for special permission you must write to:

Chief Veterinary Officer
Reykjavik, Iceland.

INDIA

Your pet dog or cat can be taken to India without any special import permits. It is necessary to have with you a health certificate for your pet that has been issued by your vet and certified by the federal veterinarian for your state. (You will find the addresses of the federal vets listed at the end of this chapter.) We have been unable to obtain information as to the procedure for obtaining gurus for animals.

INDONESIA

Your pet should have been vaccinated against rabies and you should have a health certificate attesting to the good health of your pet before you enter Indonesia. The following parts of Indonesia *prohibit* the entry of dogs, cats and monkeys: Molucca Islands, Residency of West Kalimantan (formerly West Borneo), Lesser Sunda Islands, Madura, Residency of Bengkulu (South Sumatra), Residency of Lampung (South Sumatra), Residency of Palembang (South Sumatra), Residency of Djambi (Southeast Sumatra), islands of West Sumatra, and the Residency of Riau (East Sumatra).

IRAN

To enter Iran with your pet it must have a health certificate made out by a vet. This then must be notarized and then legalized by the nearest Iranian Consulate or by the Iranian Embassy in Washington, D.C. The fee for legalization is $2.10.

IRAQ

Your dog or cat should have both rabies and distemper shots. The certificates attesting to these vaccinations should be sent to the federal vet for your state for certification. (For a list of the federal vets, see the end of this chapter.) When these documents have been returned to you, send them to the nearest Iraqi Consulate or to the Iraqi Embassy in Washington, D.C., for legalization. This should cost about $1. This done, you and your cat and/or dog are ready to see Baghdad.

IRELAND

The procedure for taking a dog or cat into Ireland is exactly the same as that given under the United Kingdom. The differences are only the addresses of the ministries, Carrying Agents and kennels. In the case of Ireland, because the lists are so much shorter, we can be quite complete. The importation form can be obtained from any Irish Consulate. It should be sent to

The Secretary
Department of Agriculture and Fisheries (Veterinary Section)
121 Lower Baggot Street
Dublin 2, Ireland

Carrying Agents

Coras Iompair Eireann	Coras Iompair Eireann
Transport House	Kent Station
Bachelor's Walk	Cork
Dublin 1	

Quarantine Kennels

For dogs	*For cats*
Wheatfield Malahide	Warren Villa
Dublin	Sutton
Mr. H. G. McDowell, MRCVS	Dublin
	Mr. H. G. McDowell, MRCVS

ISRAEL

A health certificate is required when taking a dog or a cat into Israel. Made out by your vet, it should state that the pet is in good health and shows no suspicion of rabies. It must also include the information that the state in which you and your pet live has been free from rabies for at least 6 months and that your pet has not roamed into a rabies-infested area during that time. A blood test must be taken *within 1 month* prior to arrival in Israel indicating that the animal is free of leptospirae. Make sure your vet includes a description of your pet (sex, age, color and breed) and the date of inoculation against rabies. When he signs the certificate (on his official stationery) he should include his license number. Then send the certificate to the federal vet for your state for legalization. (The addresses of the federal veterinarians will be found at the end of this chapter.)

ITALY

Have your vet, on his official stationery, make out a certificate that states the sex, breed, color and name of your pet. Also include the date of its rabies shot and the type of vaccine used. The vet should also examine the dog or cat and certify that it is free from any clinical signs of disease. This certificate is *valid for 30 days* prior to entry. Have the vet include a short statement that he is duly licensed to practice and give his license number. *Avanti!*

IVORY COAST

You will need both a health certificate and proof of rabies inoculation for your dog or cat.

JAMAICA

You cannot take your pet to Jamaica unless, of course, you want to first *put it in quarantine in the United Kingdom for 6 months.*

JAPAN

Your vet must give you a health certificate for your pet and proof of inoculation against rabies. These papers must then be sent to the federal vet for your state (addresses of the federal vets will be found at the end of this chapter) for validation. These certificates should be *more than 1 month and less than 150 days old* when you arrive in Japan.

NOTE: While there is an *official quarantine period of 2 weeks* for dogs, they are generally passed right through customs. There is no official quarantine for cats.

JORDAN

There is a *6-week quarantine* at your expense when you take a dog or a cat into Jordan. To be eligible for the quarantine your pet will have had to be inoculated with rabies vaccine *not less than 30 days or more than 1 year* before leaving home. The certificate attesting to the rabies inoculation should include the type of vaccine used, its number and manufacturer's name, and the date of manufacture. These items are usually found on the standard form you get from a vet when you have your pet vaccinated.

KENYA

You will have to get an import permit before you can go into Kenya with your pet. This is obtained from the

> Ministry of Agriculture and Animal Husbandry
> Veterinary Research Laboratory
> P.O. Kabete, Kenya

Be sure that your dog or cat has been inoculated against rabies.

KOREA

There is a *21-day quarantine* for dogs and cats in Korea. Your pets must have been vaccinated against rabies. The vaccination certificate should be validated by the federal vet for your state. (A list of these vets is found at the end of this chapter.) The points of entry for quarantine are the port of Pusan and Suyong Airport and Kimpo Airport (Seoul). There is a minimal charge. (Of course if you are spending a short time in Korea and then traveling on to a country where there is no quarantine, you can leave your pet at the quarantine kennel for less than the prescribed time and just pick it up on departure.)

LEBANON

When entering Lebanon with your pet, you need a certificate from your vet stating that the dog or cat is in good health and a notification that the animal has been inoculated with a rabies vaccine *not more than 3 months* prior to entry.

These documents should be sent to the federal veterinarian for your state for validation. (Addresses for the federal vets will be found at the end of this chapter.) When they have been returned to you, they must be sent to the nearest Lebanese Consulate for legalization. Their fee for legalization of both documents is $5.

Lesotho

At least *30 days* before your pet enters Lesotho, it must be vaccinated with an anti-rabies serum. Have the certificate attesting to this legalized by the federal veterinarian for your state. (A listing of the federal vets is found at the end of this chapter.) This certificate is valid for up to 3 years. Then apply for an entry permit from:

> Director of Veterinary Services
> P.O. Box 24
> Maseru, Lesotho.

Liberia

Once you have taken your pet to the vet and gotten from him a certificate showing that it has been inoculated with a rabies vaccine and that it is in good health, you must apply for an import permit from the Liberian Consulate nearest you or from the Liberian Embassy in Washington, D.C.

Libya

You will need a certificate showing that your pet has received its rabies shots and is in good health. That's all.

Luxembourg

Regulations are the same as for Belgium.

Mali

You need proof that your pet has had its rabies shots and is in good health. Then you are ready to enter Mali.

MALTA

Malta has a *6-month quarantine*. Pets other than dogs or cats (parakeets, for example) do not have to be quarantined and need no special documents. There is, however, an import duty of 20%—so make sure you can show your pet's value.

MARTINIQUE—See Caribbean Islands

MAURITIUS

There is a *six-month quarantine* for dogs and cats. If you are planning this, you need permission from:

> Ministry of Agriculture and National Resources
> Port Louis, Mauritius

MEXICO

First make sure that your dog or cat has been inoculated with rabies vaccine and has received distemper shots. Next you will have to take it to a vet and get a health certificate. This certificate must be made out in *duplicate* and include your name and address, description of your four-footed friend, the number of the rabies vaccine used, and a statement that the beast does not have either an infectious or contagious disease. The vet must sign this in his own hand and don't forget to see that the date is clear. With this bit of paper work done, you then send it off to the Mexican Consulate and for the small fee of $4 you can get the papers legalized. Then it's south of the border.

MONACO

If you are not entering Monaco from Australia or New Zealand, you will need a certificate showing that your pet has been inoculated with a rabies vaccine *not less than 1 month or more than 6 months* before entry into Monaco.

Morocco

No sooner than 15 days before leaving for Morocco, take your dog or cat to a vet and have him add a health certificate to the papers showing that it has been inoculated with a rabies vaccine. These papers should then be notarized and sent on to the nearest Moroccan Consulate or the Moroccan Embassy in Washington, D.C. They will charge you $5 for legalizing the papers.

Nepal

You will need a certificate showing that your dog or cat has been inoculated with rabies vaccine *more than 1 month* before departure, and *no later than 12 months earlier* if nervous-tissue vaccine was used. If chicken-embryo vaccine has been used then the shot is good for a period of 36 months. The certificate should include the manufacturer's name, the number of the vaccine and what type it was. These items are usually printed on the certificate the vet gave you when your pet was inoculated. You will also have to make sure that the dog or cat has had all its distemper shots.

That's all you will need for cats. For dogs you will also need a health certificate stating that the pooch *doesn't* have:

    Aujeszky's disease
    distemper
    leishmaniasis
    leptospirosis
    rabies

That's all folks. . . .

Netherlands

Regulations are the same as for Belgium.

Netherlands Antilles—See Caribbean Islands

Nevis—See Caribbean Islands

NEW ZEALAND

Well, dear reader, if you haven't gone through the quarantine procedure in Ireland or the United Kingdom you aren't going to take your cat or dog to New Zealand. No exceptions at all.

NICARAGUA

You need a health certificate from your vet and proof of rabies shots in order for your pet to be allowed to enter Nicaragua. You must also apply for an import permit from the

Ministerio de Agricultura y Ganadería
Managua, Nicaragua

This permit costs $10 and is *valid for 30 days*. When you apply for the permit, enclose copies of the health and rabies certificates. If nervous-tissue vaccine was used, the shot must be given *at least 30 days* prior to entry; if chick-embryo vaccine was used, it must be given *at least 60 days* before your planned arrival.

NIGERIA

Your pet should have its rabies shots and an examination by your vet. When you have the documents attesting to your pet's good health and inoculation, send them on to the federal vet for your state. (A list of these vets will be found at the end of this chapter.) When these papers have been returned to you, you must send them on to Nigeria for an import permit. Write to the

Director of Federal Department of Veterinary Research
Vom, Jos
Nigeria

When you have received your reply from Nigeria, the formalities are finished and you are ready to leave.

NORTHERN IRELAND—See United Kingdom

NORWAY

You are not permitted to take any living animal into Norway, BUT you may be granted special permission to take your pet into Norway if you apply to the

> Ministry of Agriculture
> Veterinaerdirektortet
> Oslo-Dep., Norway

You should include information about the kind and number of animals you want to bring, how they will arrive in Norway, and the time they will arrive (this last point can be a rough estimate). If you are given a license to import your pet you then must have a health certificate from your vet. Then your pet will be examined when it arrives in Norway *and* put into *quarantine for 4 months!* There are no exceptions to quarantine regulations.

OKINAWA

Your family is allowed to bring in only 2 pets that are older than 2 months (never mind numerology!). Now, if you are taking 1 or 2 pets you have to get a health certificate for them from a vet within *10 days* before departure. This should state that their health is good and that they have been inoculated against rabies. (This has to be made out in *triplicate* but at least there is no Catch-22.)

If your dog or cat was vaccinated with a nervous-tissue vaccine, the shot is valid for 12 months, whereas if chicken-embryo vaccine was used, it will be good for 36 months. In either case, the shot must have been administered *at least 30 days* before arrival.

PAKISTAN

If you plan to travel to Pakistan with your pet dog or cat you must first get a health certificate from your vet. This should then be legalized by the federal veterinarian for your state. (A list of the federal veterinarians will be found at the end of this chapter.) We recommend that you check to see that your pet has a valid rabies vaccination, and if not you could see to that when you're at the vet's getting the health certificate. (While rabies vaccination is not required for entry into Pakistan, a pet lacking one will be vaccinated at entry.) Once you have the legalized health certificate, send it along to the Office of the Imports and Exports Control Organization at your point of entry into Pakistan. They will issue an Import Permit and you should then have no trouble taking your pet along.

PANAMA

There is a *180-day quarantine* in Panama applicable to both dogs and cats. If you are planning to put your pet in quarantine, you will also need health and rabies certificates made out by your vet. These certificates must be sent to your nearest Panamanian Consulate for legalization.

PARAGUAY

Have your vet make out a certificate stating that your dog or cat has had its rabies shots and is in good health.

PERU

Your pet must have both rabies and distemper shots. The certificate your vet makes out attesting to this should be made out in *duplicate*. This must then be legalized by the nearest Peruvian Consulate.

PHILIPPINES

A short time before you're ready to leave, take your pet to a vet and have it inoculated against rabies and also have the vet examine it so that he can make out a health certificate stating that it is free from dangerous and communicable diseases. If you don't have rabies and health certificates your animal may be placed in quarantine for 10 days. Have these documents certified by the federal vet for your state. (A list of these vets appears at the end of this chapter.)

POLAND

Just take along a health certificate and proof of vaccination against rabies.

PORTUGAL

Your dog or cat must be vaccinated with rabies serum before entering Portugal. The certificate showing that this has been done should be *good for 1 year*. When you have gotten this certificate from your vet, it must be notarized. After notarization the certificate should be sent on to the nearest Portuguese Consulate for validation. Once this has been returned to you, you are able to enter Portugal without further problems.

PUERTO RICO

Your pet must be inoculated against rabies *more than 30 days* before departure for Puerto Rico. You will also need a health certificate from your vet stating that there have been no cases of rabies within 50 miles of your home for a period of at least 6 months. The rabies and health certificates should then be sent to the federal vet for your state for validation. (A list of these vets will be found at the end of this chapter.) When the papers are returned you will be ready to go on your Puerto Rican holiday.

RHODESIA

Your vet must make out a health certificate for your pet which conforms to the following regulations; your pet must be in good health with no evidence of external parasites or contagious disease; if you live in an area which has been rabies-free for the past six months, your pet must have had its rabies shots *more than 30 days* and *less than 36 months* (*12 months* for cats) before entry; if there has been rabies within 50 miles of your home in the prior six months, rabies shots must be given *more than six months* but *less than 36 months* (*12 months* for cats) before entry. If your pet has had its rabies shots and they've expired (not the pets—the shots), the pet will be admitted 30 days after revaccination. If your dog is too young for its shots, you must notify the veterinary officer when you arrive. You then must bring it for its shots when it is three months old. No unvaccinated cats will be allowed. If your pet doesn't conform to these regulations, it will be quarantined at your expense until six months have passed since its vaccination.

ROMANIA

The only thing your pet will need for entry into Romania is a health certificate from your vet. It should also state that your pet has had its rabies shots.

RWANDA

Take along proof that your animal has had its inoculation for rabies. That's it.

SABA—See Caribbean Islands

ST. EUSTATIUS—See Caribbean Islands

ST. KITTS—See Caribbean Islands

ST. LUCIA—See Caribbean Islands

St. Maarten—See Caribbean Islands

St. Vincent—See Caribbean Islands

Saudi Arabia

Have with you a certificate stating that your pet has been inoculated against rabies and all other contagious diseases.

Scotland—See United Kingdom

Senegal

Have your vet examine your pet and issue a good-health certificate. You also will need proof that your pet has had its rabies shots.

Sierra Leone

You must apply for an import permit from the

> Chief Veterinary Officer
> Ministry of Agriculture and Natural Resources
> Freetown, Sierra Leone

Your pet must be examined by your vet and found to be in good health. It must also be inoculated against rabies. Cats need vaccination against feline enteritis. Dogs need, in addition to rabies shots, vaccinations against distemper, hard pad, hepatitis and leptospirosis.

Singapore

Dogs and cats from the United States are given rabies vaccination on arrival. They are then put in *quarantine for a minimum of 30 days* at the Government Animal Quarantine Station, Jalan Kimia, Jurong, Singapore. If you have a puppy or kitten less than 4 months old, it will be put in quarantine and at 4 months of age it will be given its rabies shot and kept in quarantine for at least another 30 days. Pregnant dogs are not admitted.

You must apply for an import license at least 2 weeks before your pet will arrive. This costs $10 (Singapore currency). You request quarantine accommodations at the same time. Apply to the

Director of Primary Production
City Veterinary Centre
40, Kampong Java Road
Singapore, 9

If you have a pet other than a dog or a cat you must still apply for an import license. Their reply will concern what other papers and/or procedures are involved before your pet can enter Singapore. The costs for quarantine are $2 per day for cats, $2 per day for dogs weighing less than 40 pounds and $2.50 for dogs weighing more than 40 pounds. This includes the price of feeding. Each rabies vaccination costs $10.

South Africa

To take your dog, cat or bird into South Africa you must apply for an import permit. This can be obtained from any South African Consulate or from the

Chief, Division of Veterinary Field Services
Private Bag 138
Pretoria, South Africa

This application should be filled out and returned to the officer in South Africa 6 to 8 weeks before your planned departure. Your dog or cat must be vaccinated with an approved rabies vaccine. These are Flury, Kelev, Pasteur, Pitman Moore and Vom. For dogs the vaccination must have taken place *more than 180 days and less than 36 months* prior to entry. For cats it must be *more than 180 days but less than 1 year* prior to entry. The vet should include in the certificate the date of vaccination as well as the type and manufacturer's

One lady & one bird to Madrid, please.

number. You must also get a health certificate from the vet stating that the animal appears to be healthy, free from external parasites (get the flea powder ready!), and that it has no infectious or contagious diseases. It also must be found free of histoplasmosis. This must be *within 14 days* before departure. Also included should be information that, to the best of your vet's knowledge, your pet has not been in contact with rabid animals.

If your dog or cat hasn't been vaccinated or is less than 3 months old, it will be vaccinated upon arrival and put in quarantine for 180 days. You will have to pay all the expenses so incurred. The quarantine stations are at Jan Smuts Airport (near Johannesburg), Durban and Cape Town. If your pet has been vaccinated but the vaccination was less than 180 days before entry, then it will be put in quarantine for a length of time calculated as the difference between the date of its inoculation and 180 days.

NOTE: En route to South Africa by plane, your pet must not be let out of its kennel. The plane's officer must attest to this. If you're going by ship, then you should not let the pet off the ship until you're in South Africa and a ship's officer must attest to this.

SOVIET UNION—See Union of Soviet Socialist Republics

SPAIN

To take a pet dog or cat into Spain you must get a certificate of good health from your vet. This certificate should include a statement to the effect that your pet is free from any contagious disease. If you are taking your dog, the certificate should also state that it has been successfully inoculated with rabies vaccine. This document must be certified at the Spanish Consulate nearest your home. The consular fee for this is $5.45.

SUDAN

You must apply for permission to bring your pet into Sudan. This is obtained from the

> Ministry of Animal Resources
> Khartoum, Sudan

This application costs 40 cents. If you simply don't have the time to make application, it is possible to get permission on arrival.

Obtain a health certificate as well as proof of rabies and distemper shots. These shots must have been administered *less than 3 years but not less than 1 month* before you plan to enter. Send these papers (or copies of them) along with your request for entry permit.

When your pet arrives in Sudan it should be in a closed kennel and it will then be examined to make sure that it is in good health.

SURINAM

Regulations are the same as for Belgium.

SWEDEN

There is a *4-month quarantine* for dogs and cats entering Sweden from the United States. If you wish to put your dog or cat in quarantine you must first apply for an import license. This application is sent to:

> Veterinärstyrelsen (Royal Veterinary Board)
> Fack 10360
> Stockholm 3, Sweden

You should allow at least a month before departure for the acquisition of the license and other arrangements. You will have to make sure that there is space for your pet at a quarantine kennel. For this information write to:

The Quarantine Veterinarian
Board of Health
(Hälsovårdsnämnden)
Göteborg (Stockholm, Malmö, Hälsingborg or Hapa-
randa) Sweden

The cost of quarantine is about 5 Swedish kronor per day.

Not more than 10 days before departure you must have your vet certify that your pet is healthy and not suspected of being a carrier of any communicable diseases. The certificate should also include the information that your dog has been tested and found free of any signs of infection by leptospirae (spirochetes). Cats need only be certified in good health and free from infectious diseases. This certificate should then be legalized by the federal vet in your state. (A list of federal vets will be found at the end of this chapter.)

At least 24 hours before your pet's arrival in Sweden, you must notify the veterinarian at quarantine of the time of your pet's arrival and the mode of transport used. You must also include the plane's flight number or ship's name if either of these is used.

When your pet arrives it will be examined immediately to make sure that it is indeed in apparent good health. It is then taken to quarantine either in its sealed crate or in the care of the vet. When it arrives at quarantine it will be tested again for leptospirae (if it's a dog). If, while in quarantine, your pet develops leptospirosis or other infectious diseases it may be destroyed by the government. It will definitely be destroyed if it contracts rabies. Check when you apply for an import license so that you can avoid destruction of your pet and arrange for its export in the event of contraction of diseases other than rabies.

All expenses incurred while your pet is on the way to and in quarantine kennel must be paid by you, the owner of the loyal and wonderful beast.

NOTE: If you are simply passing through Sweden with your pet dog or cat you may do so by keeping the pet in a cage or box. It may not stay at an airport stopover more than 24 hours. If you are passing through by car, ship or train, the Swedish Customs will seal the cage or kennel and this will remain so until you have left the country.

SWITZERLAND

To enter Switzerland with your dog or cat you must have with you a certificate that your pet has been inoculated with a rabies vaccine *not less than 30 days or more than 1 year* before entry. The certificate should contain your name and address, a description of your pet (its breed, color, sex and age), date of the vaccination, manufacturer's name and the serial number of the vaccine, and the veterinarian's stamp and signature. It should, of course, also state that your pet is in good health. This should then be sent to the federal vet for legalization. (The addresses of the federal vets for each state are given at the end of this chapter.)

NOTE: If you are just passing through Switzerland, this document is not required.

SYRIA

Your pet will need a health certificate as well as proof that it has had its rabies and distemper shots.

TAHITI

Regulations are the same as for France.

TANZANIA

Your pet will need a rabies inoculation and a health certificate. You must apply for an import permit from the

Chief Veterinary Officer
P.O. Box 9152
Dar es Salaam, Tanzania

THAILAND

Your pet should have been vaccinated against rabies and you will have to have proof of this. Then you must apply for an import permit from the

> Department of Animal Husbandry
> Paholyothin Road
> Bangkok, Thailand

While the import permit costs only 25 cents, there is a 30% duty based on the value of your pet when you enter Thailand.

TOGO

Your dog or cat should have a rabies inoculation and you should have a certificate stating that your pet is in good health. Consult your vet about the need for vaccination against tropical diseases. The dog or cat will be examined upon arrival at the airport at Lomé by an officer of the Animal Health Department. If all the necessary vaccinations have been administered, you will be allowed to enter immediately. If not, the Animal Health Department will administer the shots and will keep your pet *in quarantine* for observation for up to *2 weeks*.

TRINIDAD AND TOBAGO

There is a *quarantine period of at least 6 months*. You must notify the

> Veterinary Officer
> North
> c/o St. Joseph Farm
> Trinidad

at least 24 hours before your animal will arrive. Then your pet will be picked up, examined and put in quarantine. You should first send to the above officer for permission to bring your pet in and inform him of your planned time of arrival so that he will make sure that there are quarantine facilities available. Make sure that your animal arrives in a well-secured kennel.

TUNISIA

When you enter Tunisia with your dog you must have a rabies vaccination certificate dated *more than 1 month but not more than 6 months* prior to entry. For both dogs and cats you will need a certificate of good health from your vet.

TURKEY

In this case the paper you need should be made out in *duplicate!* Have your vet give you a combined health certificate and vaccination against rabies statement. This should be notarized and certified by your local county clerk. (If the paper was issued by an Armed Forces vet, you need not have it notarized or certified.) Then send the paper—*in duplicate*—to the nearest Turkish Consulate for legalization. Their fee is $3.50. They would also like you to enclose a stamped, self-addressed envelope.

UGANDA

You must get an import permit before you can take your pet into Uganda. This can be gotten from the

> Commissioner
> Veterinary Department
> P.O. Box 7141
> Kampala, Uganda

You should also see that your pet has been given its rabies shots *not less than 30 days or more than 3 years* before its departure for Uganda, and that it has been examined by a vet and found to be in good health *within 10 days* of its departure. If your animal is to arrive in Uganda by plane, make arrangements with the airline so that the Master of the Aircraft can furnish a certificate stating that your pet has had no contact with other animals during the flight. If it is to arrive by ship, you must arrange for an International Movement permit. This can be gotten at either Dar es Salaam or Mombassa from the Transit Veterinary Department.

UNION OF SOVIET SOCIALIST REPUBLICS

Once you have been to your vet and gotten a health and rabies vaccination certificate for your pet it will be allowed to enter the Soviet Union. Before you plan your trip with your pet, be sure to check page 231 for the regulations concerning pet travel *within* the U.S.S.R.

UNITED ARAB REPUBLIC

Once your pet has been vaccinated against rabies and has been examined by the vet and found in good health, you are able to enter the U.A.R.

UNITED KINGDOM

This information will be of interest if you are planning a long stay in Britain. A *6-month quarantine* pretty much excludes a more casual traveler-*cum*-pet expedition. Six months is the minimum time for quarantine in Britain. Should any outbreak of rabies occur while your pet is in quarantine, the period can be extended to as long as 1 year. If you do put your pet in quarantine you will need no special documents from your vet as the animal will be revaccinated at the quarantine kennel. The paper work you have thus saved is all to the good because importation requires several steps, each one of which requires correspondence.

First, apply for an import license from one of the following:

(a) *For Scotland*
The Secretary
Department of Agriculture and Fisheries for Scotland
Chesser House
500 Gorgie Road
Edinburgh EH11 3 AW, Scotland

(b) *For the remainder of Great Britain*
The Secretary
Ministry of Agriculture, Fisheries and Food-Animal Health Division
Hook Rise South
Tolworth, Surbiton
Surrey, England

An import application form can also be obtained from the British Information Services, 845 Third Avenue, New York City 10022.

Now, you hold on to the form because, before a license will be granted, you must arrange with a licensed British Carrying Agent to have your pet picked up at its point of landing and transported to the quarantine kennel. They will provide a carrying kennel for your pet. If you already have such a kennel or will get one in order to ship your dog or cat to Britain, check with the Carrying Agent to make sure that they will accept it.

More or less simultaneously you should write to an approved quarantine kennel to reserve a place for your pet. You will see below a brief list of approved Carrying Agents and quarantine kennels. For a complete list, contact either British Information or the ministries. Be sure to ask for the fees charged by the carriers and by the kennels. When you have completed arrangements with these agencies, they will notify the ministry of the arrangements. Now you can finish the application for the import license and send it off to the ministry. They will grant the license to the Carrying Agent and will notify you of the license number and will in effect give you the go-ahead signal.

NOTE: You need not know the exact time of importation or the exact place in order to have the license processed. You can give the carrier and kennel approximate dates and send in the form and later inform them of the exact date and place. Remember that all expenses will be paid by the pet owner. And if you plan to visit your dog or cat while it's quarantined, don't forget to make these arrangements while you're booking the kennel.

NOTE: If you are planning a long stay in Britain and so are considering putting your dog or cat in quarantine you might like to know that the British are very fond of animals and you can reasonably expect that your pet will be well treated while it is in the kennel.

Carrying Agents

Air Pets Oceanic
(London)
Willowslea Farm
Spout Lane
Stanwell, Staines
Middlesex, England

Arbuckle Smith & Co., Ltd.
91 Mitchell Street
Glasgow C1, Scotland

I.F.A. Ltd.
Room 2/3
Building 9
Manchester Airport
Manchester, England

Anglo Overseas
Transport Co., Ltd.
16 New Street
London EC 2, England

Aviation Quarantine
Deliveries
Long Lane
Stanwell
Middlesex, England

Miss C. J. Sherren
Animal Taxi
7 Eastcliffe
Dover
Kent, England

Quarantine Kennels

Veterinary Infirmary
Cowley Road
Uxbridge
Middlesex, England
Mr. M. O'Higgins, Prop.

Willowslea Farm
Kennels
Spout Lane
Stanwell, Staines
Middlesex, England
Mr. J. H. Woodward, Prop.

Tower Dog Home
Liberton Drive
Edinburgh 9, Scotland
Capt. A. K. Cameron,
BSc, MRCVS

Partingdale Manor
Partingdale Lane
Mill Hill
London, N.W. 7,
England
Mr. K. G. D. and Mrs.
O. W. Evans, MsRCVS

The White House
Long Acre Farm
Long Lane
Stanwell
Middlesex, England
Mr. H. A. Scott, Prop.

URUGUAY

Your dog or cat must have rabies shots and be examined by a vet and found in good health. When you've received the documents from the vet that attest to this, send them off to the federal vet for your state. (A list of these vets will be found at the end of this chapter.) When these papers are returned to you, take them or send them to the nearest consular office of Uruguay, where they will be legalized. The fee for consular legalization is $10.50. They will return them in the next day's mail and you will be set to travel.

VENEZUELA

To enter Venezuela with your dog or cat you must get a health certificate from a vet. You should also have proof that your animal has been inoculated against rabies and dysentery. This latter requirement might indicate that you are not the only being who should stick to bottled water!

Virgin Islands

You must get a health certificate from your vet that should be made out on an official state form. The certificate should make clear that your pet is free from any sort of disease and doesn't live in an area where there is a rabies quarantine. Dogs and cats must have had rabies shots *not less than 2 weeks or more than 6 months* before their departure. The health certificate should then be sent on to the federal vet for your state to be legalized. (A list of federal vets appears at the end of this chapter.) The certificate is *valid for 30 days*.

Wales—See United Kingdom

West Indies

Most of the islands do not permit pets.

Yemen

Dogs and cats are *not* permitted to land in Yemen.

Yugoslavia

You need a certificate stating that your dog or cat has been inoculated against rabies *15 to 180 days* prior to arrival in Yugoslavia, and you're off!

Zambia

Your pet must have an import permit before it can enter Zambia. Send to the

> Director of Veterinary Services
> P.B. RW60
> Lusaka, Zambia

If your dog has not had a rabies shot, it will receive one within 3 months of arrival in Zambia. Otherwise all it needs is a health certificate from your vet.

FEDERAL VETERINARIANS

Eastern Area

Dr. Walter Ferrall
254 Post Office Building
135 High Street
Hartford, *Connecticut* 06101

Dr. L. T. Fisher
Post Office Box 399
109 Bridge Street
Frankfort, *Kentucky* 40601

Dr. C. W. Wilder
U.S. Post Office & Federal
Building
40 Western Avenue
Augusta, *Maine* 04330

Dr. W. C. Ferrall
802 Customhouse Building
Boston, *Massachusetts* 02109

Dr. C. L. Hendee
5th Floor, Lewis Cass
Building
Lansing, *Michigan* 48913

Dr. R. L. Alkire
Post Office Box 938
Health & Agriculture Building
John Fitch Plaza
Trenton, *New Jersey* 08605

Dr. R. J. Rodgers
Building 8, State Campus
Albany, *New York* 12226

Dr. P. H. Kramer
Room 448
Old Post Office Building
Columbus, *Ohio* 43215

Dr. G. T. Mainwaring
Post Office Box 2065
2301 North Cameron Street
Harrisburg, *Pennsylvania*
17105

Dr. R. M. Scott
State Agricultural Building
Montpelier, *Vermont* 05602

Dr. H. D. White
3404 Federal Office Building
500 Quarrier Street
Charleston, *West Virginia*
25301

Midwestern Area

Dr. Milo L. Johnson
Post Office Box 2149
100½ East Washington Street
Springfield, *Illinois* 62701

Dr. L. R. Barnes
311 West Washington Street
Room 210
Indianapolis, *Indiana* 46204

Dr. G. W. Spangler
Room 877 Federal Building
210 Walnut Street
Des Moines, *Iowa* 50309

Dr. D. O. Manley
Post Office Box 1518
536 Jefferson Street
Topeka, *Kansas* 66601

Dr. D. F. Werring
555 Wabasha Street
St. Paul, *Minnesota* 55102

Dr. Robert Morgan
Post Office Box 1027
203-205 Post Office Building
Jefferson City, *Missouri* 65101

Dr. E. H. Nordstrom
Post Office Box 1866
303 Farmers Mutual
Insurance Building
1220 J Street
Lincoln, *Nebraska* 68501

Dr. M. B. Hoffman
Post Office Box 639
Room 222 Federal Building
220 East Rosser Avenue
Bismarck, *North Dakota* 58501

Dr. E. M. Joneschild
Post Office Box 758
Room 317
New U.S. Courthouse &
Post Office
Pierre, *South Dakota* 57501

Dr. A. A. Erdmann
Hill Farms State Office
Building
4802 Sheboygan Avenue—
Room 220B
Madison, *Wisconsin* 53702

Dr. W. M. Reynolds
Post Office Box 825
2120 Capitol Avenue
Post Office & Courthouse,
Room 8007
Cheyenne, *Wyoming* 82001

Dr. J. H. Slack
200 Steamboat Block
616 Helena Avenue
Helena, *Montana* 59601

Southern Area

Dr. B. C. Swindle
Post Office Box 1749
421 South McDonough Street
Montgomery, *Alabama* 36103

Dr. Paul Becton
Post Office Box 3548
Room 5506 Federal Building
Little Rock, *Arkansas* 72203

Dr. W. L. Rehkemper
State Board of Agriculture
Building
Post Office Drawer D
Dover, *Delaware* 19901

Dr. J. B. Healy
Box Number 35028
480 New Federal Building
400 West Bay Street
Jacksonville, *Florida* 32202

Dr. C. J. Mikel
Room 1030 Title Building
30 Pryor Street, S.W.
Atlanta, *Georgia* 30303

Dr. F. E. Henderson
Post Office Box 1391
New Post Office Building
750 Florida Boulevard
Baton Rouge, *Louisiana* 70821

Dr. P. M. Eppele, Acting
Room 510 Hartwick Building
4321 Hartwick Road
College Park, *Maryland* 20740

Dr. O. L. Kelsey
Post Office Box 1120
400 Milner Building
Corner Lamar & Pearl Streets
Jackson, *Mississippi* 39205

Dr. W. W. Harkins
Post Office Box 2656
320 Agricultural Building
Raleigh, *North Carolina* 27603

Dr. R. L. Evinger
General Post Office Box 3488
6th Floor, Hato Rey Building
Ponce de Leon Avenue
& Bolivia Street
Hato Rey, *Puerto Rico* 00919

Dr. C. E. Boyd
Post Office Box 1771
Columbia, *South Carolina*
29202

Dr. W .W. Bird
Post Office Box 510
548 U.S. Courthouse
Nashville, *Tennessee* 37202

Dr. E. C. Roukema
Room 204
1444 East Main Street
Richmond, *Virginia* 23219

Western Area

Dr. Dean Price
Room 28 Federal Building
Anchorage, *Alaska* 99501

Dr. O. D. Corson
Post Office Box 7397
4004 North 7th Street
Phoenix, *Arizona* 85006

Dr. J. H. Wommack
650 Capitol Mall, Room 8566
Sacramento, *California* 95814

Dr. R. W. Gerding
13037 Federal Building,
U.S. Courthouse
1961 Stout Street
Denver, *Colorado* 80202

Dr. W. W. Thomas
1481 South King Street,
Room 436
Honolulu, *Hawaii* 96814

Dr. A. P. Schneider
716 Idaho Street
Boise, *Idaho* 83702

Dr. C. R. Watson
1395 Haskell Street
Suite B
Reno, *Nevada* 89502

Dr. L. N. Miller, Jr.
1421 Federal Building
200 Northwest 4
Oklahoma City, *Oklahoma*
73102

Dr. O. J. Halverson
494 State Street, Room 203
Salem, *Oregon* 97301

Dr. E. S. Cox
Room 301
702 Colorado Street
Austin, *Texas* 78701

Dr. S. C. Gartman
Post Office 969
Moore Air Force Base
Mission, *Texas* 78572

Dr. J. E. Rasmussen
Post Office Box 11429
5237 Federal Building
125 South State Street
Salt Lake City, *Utah* 84111

Dr. J. K. Atwell
Post Office Box 87
201 Union Avenue Building
120 East Union Avenue
Olympia, *Washington* 98501

Dr. R. P. Pyles
Post Office Box 464
4010 New Federal
Office Building
517 Gold Avenue
Albuquerque, *New Mexico*
87103

INTERNATIONAL TRAVEL
BY PLANE AND SHIP

This chapter gives a survey by airline and ship line of the regulations, costs and services provided by each. As you will see, it is often cheaper to take your pet along than to leave it at home. As we have already said, it is much more enjoyable. We'll first answer some basic questions about shipment.

Can Your Pet Fly with You in the Cabin?

You will find in the breakdown by airline which ones permit pets in the cabin. If an airline does permit pets in the cabin, they must be small. While size is relative and your pet lion may be small in comparison to a rhino, let us agree that what the airlines mean by a small pet is more like a house cat, hamster or a miniature poodle.

If the airline will take your pet in the cabin, it must be in a well-secured and well-ventilated container and you will pay for it at the excess-baggage rate.

The number of pets allowed in the cabin of the aircraft is fixed and determined by international agreement. If your airline permits such travel, make your reservations early. If other people with small pets have reserved space before you, you won't be able to get your pet in the cabin on a given flight.

Do Airlines Sell or Rent Carrying Cases and Kennels?

You will find under the heading for each airline whether it sells kennels or rents them and whether it provides cardboard carriers.

How to Send Your Pet as Air Cargo

If your pet cannot accompany you in the cabin, you can take it along in the baggage section of the plane. This section is heated and pressurized in the same way that your cabin is. Your pet, of course, must be in a well-secured, well-ventilated sturdy kennel. Make sure that any kennel you buy is roomy enough for your pet. Dogs must have enough room to stand freely, turn around and lie down. (Greyhounds are the exception—they must not be permitted to turn.)

When shipping a pet as cargo there are two alternatives open. (Exceptions will be noted where appropriate.) Your pet can be taken to the departure terminal with you and loaded on the plane from there. You are then charged the excess-baggage rate. When you arrive at your destination your pet will be delivered to you in the same place that your baggage is delivered. You should allow yourself enough time to put the kennel together if this is necessary. Otherwise, when shipping your pet as excess baggage, you get to the airport at the same time you would if traveling without a pet.

You can ship your pet at the regular air-cargo rate for pets (which is typically almost half that of excess baggage). This is done by taking your pet to the cargo building at the airport. While the requirements vary among airlines, the average time before departure for pet delivery is about 3 hours. You leave your pet there and when you arrive at your destination you must go to the cargo building and retrieve your pet. This, of course, adds several hours to your trip and to your pet's, but it does save quite a bit of money.

What Does It Cost?

Pets shipped in the cabin and pets loaded at the departure terminal as cargo are charged the excess-baggage rate in many cases. This rate is 1% of the one-way first-class air fare to your destination per kilo. That is, for every 2.2 pounds of combined pet and kennel weight you will pay the 1% charge.

The air-cargo rate is not figured on a percentage basis and so generally you must check with the cargo department of the airline for the exact cost of transporting your pet.

NOTE: You will see that when we list the weight of various kennels there is one thing called pound weight and another called volume weight. Pound weight is figured out just by putting the kennel on a scale. The volume weight is arrived at in a slightly more obscure fashion. However, you should be aware that volume weight is the *minimum* weight you will be charged for shipment. You pay pound or volume weight depending on which is greater. So you will always pay at least the volume weight. If your pet in its kennel weighs more than the volume weight for the kennel, then the rate is figured on the combined poundage of pet plus kennel; if it weighs less than the volume weight when it's in its kennel, you will pay for the volume weight.

You will note that individual airlines arrive at shipping costs in a different manner than those above. There are cases where no matter the size or weight of your pet you pay on the basis of the price of your own ticket.

REMEMBER: While there is a category called excess-baggage rate, this refers to price and not to how much baggage you do or do not have! No matter how many pounds under the baggage allowance you find yourself, your pet's rate is *all* excess baggage.

What About Charters?

Most nonscheduled charter flights refuse to take any pets. Charter organizations that use scheduled airliners have individual policies concerning pets. Both permission to take your pet and the rates involved will vary from flight to flight, so check as early as you can with your charter organization for full details.

How Do Seeing Eye Dogs Travel?

Almost every airline permits a Seeing Eye dog to accompany its master or mistress in the cabin of the plane, regardless of the dog's size. This is a service of the airlines and there is no charge for the dog.

What About Documents?

The chapter "Instead of a Passport" lists the necessary documents for entry into various countries. Remember that when you have these health documents, import permits or quarantine arrangements, you must take them with you to the airport when you are shipping your pet. In other words, you need them for shipment as well as for entry into different countries. Cargo will refuse to accept an animal if you can't show them that you have the papers that are required for entry. Remember too that your pet's kennel should be clearly marked with your name and your pet's name and destination.

What if There Are Stopovers or Plane Changes?

If you are not flying direct to your destination you must give the cargo department of the airline you are starting out with a few extra days to plan your pet's trip. If notified in time, they will cable ahead to any other carrier used to make sure that they will be prepared for your pet. Be sure to attach

The airlines usually take good care of your pet.

your pet's leash to the outside of its kennel (when appropriate) and to attach some food and a water dish if the flight will be long. In this way the airline personnel will be able to exercise your pet and make sure that it has adequate food and water on long journeys. Most of the major airports have facilities for housing pets if, for example, they have to spend a night while waiting for a connecting flight. Cargo will inform you of the expenses involved in such an arrangement if it is necessary.

How Well Do Pets Take to Plane Travel?

The chapter "Training Your Dog or Cat to Travel" will tell you how to treat your pet for a flight and how to accustom it to travel. When I (Paula) took my shaggy dog Louie on his first flight it was a 7-hour trip to Amsterdam. I had always thought that Louie was high-strung. He shied away from loud noises, was scared of anything that even resembled a cage, and drooled. I arranged to get some dog tranquilizers from a vet, but somehow I was still worried that poor Louie would have a fearful time. Because of this I decided to ship him as excess baggage and so be able to have him put on the plane just a little while before I would board. That this would cost almost twice as much as sending him via cargo was a cruel fact of life, but at least the trip would be shortened for him. Once aboard, I worried from time to time about how he was doing down there in the baggage section (never mind that it was heated and pressurized and that there was a light). The stewardesses informed me that most pets travel better than people, but of course you know how professionally cheerful a stewardess is.

Minutes after I arrived in Amsterdam I saw Louie. There he was, sitting up in his cage, looking around and taking in the whole scene. He didn't seem any the worse for the trip at all, in fact he was energetic and curious about everything.

So much for fears and the added expense. On future flights I will send Louie via cargo. Louie was well on his way to becoming a seasoned traveler. And so was I.

A Few Words of Advice About Purchasing a Kennel

If it is at all possible (and do try to make it possible) get your pet's kennel at least a day before the flight. This is especially true if your dog is large. Often cargo agents or airline reservation personnel will assure you that their large kennel is big enough for your pet. This just is not always the case. Because pet reservations are not made through personnel specifically charged solely with this responsibility there are possible foul-ups in communication between reservation clerks and cargo personnel. You may be promised just the kennel you want and then find it doesn't exist when you are at the airport—with an hour before the flight. Of course, this is not always the case. I had the experience of making careful advance reservations for a kennel and then finding 1½ hours before flight time that not only didn't they have a kennel large enough for Louie but the people at Kennedy had never even heard of the man who was personally "taking care" of the arrangements. Fortunately, they found a cage large enough for a bear just in time.

The fact is that, as you will see in the following material, many airlines have kennels. If you are able to pick one up the day before and if your airline has erred in any way, they will have ample time to get a proper one from another airline. They are willing and able to do this, so do try to give yourself ample time. Then when you are actually ready for departure you will have nothing to worry about. Of course, once your pet has traveled by air you will probably be in possession of the right kennel and won't have to be concerned with this issue at all.

With a slight bit of advance planning, you will be able to enjoy traveling with a jet setter (I couldn't resist!).

BY PLANE

AER LINGUS—See Irish International Airlines

AEROFLOT SOVIET AIRLINES—See Pan American Airways

Pan Am handles the reservations, cargo arrangements and sale of kennels for Aeroflot.

AEROLINEAS ARGENTINAS

Cabin: No pets allowed.

Kennels: They do not sell or rent kennels.

Shipping Costs: If shipped as excess baggage (see chapter's introductory remarks for explanation), the price is 1% of the normal first-class one-way jet ticket per kilo (2.2 pounds). If sent as cargo, the rates vary with size and destination. A sample cargo rate would be $1.70 per pound (pet plus kennel) for the New York to Buenos Aires flight.

Shipping Procedure: If sent as excess baggage, take your pet to the departure terminal a half hour before you have to check in. If sent as air cargo, you must take your pet to the cargo building 6½ hours before flight time.

Insurance: Make your own arrangements because they do not sell insurance for pets.

AERONAVES DE MEXICO

Cabin: No pets allowed.

Kennels: They neither sell nor rent kennels.

Shipping Costs: If shipped as excess baggage (see chapter's introductory remarks for explanation), the rate is 1% of the normal one-way first-class jet fare per kilo (2.2 pounds). If shipped as cargo, the rate is 44 cents per pound (pet plus kennel).

Shipping Procedure: Take your pet to the cargo building 4 hours before departure time.

Insurance: You must arrange this yourself because they do not sell pet insurance.

AIR CANADA

Cabin: Only Seeing Eye dogs are permitted in the cabin. These are handled free of charge.

Kennels: If you are providing your own kennel it must be approved by their service manager at the airport. Air Canada sells Kloud Kennels (which you should request as early as possible). They come in the following sizes:

Type	Small	Medium	Large
L x W x H	17" x 11½" x 14"	24" x 15" x 21"	36" x 21" x 30"
Cost in			
U.S. Dollars	$8.50	$14.50	$22.50

Shipping Costs: The cost of shipping your pet is determined by the price of your ticket and not the size or weight of your pet. If your ticket is less than $25, your pet's fare is $4. Between $25 and $50, your pet costs $6. Between $50 and $120, pet fare is $8. Between $120 and $200, pet fare is $10. If your ticket costs $200 or more, pet transport costs $12.

Shipping Procedure: Take your pet to the check-in counter at least 3 hours before departure time.

Insurance: You must make your own arrangements because Air Canada does not sell insurance for pet transport.

AIR FRANCE

Cabin: If your pet can fit into a container no larger than 18" x 12" x 9" you can reserve a place in the cabin.

Kennels: Kennels are sold at the airports in New York, Chicago, Los Angeles, Montreal and Mexico City. The prices quoted for New York are the same in Chicago and Los Angeles. In all cases the kennels are the same sizes and are made of plywood.

Type	Small	Medium	Large
L x W x H	18″ x 12″ x 16″	24″ x 14″ x 20″	32″ x 20″ x 24″
Weight	4.5 lbs.	9.5 lbs.	17 lbs.
Cost			
N.Y.	$6.90	$8.70	$12.70
Montreal	$7 (Canadian)	$9 (Canadian)	$13 (Canadian)
Mexico City	160 pesos	190 pesos	220 pesos

Shipping Costs: If shipped as excess baggage (see chapter's introductory remarks for explanation), the rate is 1% of the one-way first-class jet fare per kilo (2.2 pounds) of the weight of your pet plus kennel. If shipped as cargo, the price varies with destination. If your pet is going from New York to Paris (for the special four-legged gourmet tour, no doubt!) the rate is $1.29 per pound (pet plus kennel).

Shipping Procedure: As always you must notify the cargo department at least a day in advance that your animal will be coming on the flight. You must take it to the cargo building (if shipped as freight) at least 4½ hours before departure. If shipped as excess baggage, take it to the departure terminal at least a half hour before you have to check in.

Insurance: Insurance costs 15 cents per $100 declared value.

AIR NEW ZEALAND—See British Overseas Airways Corporation

BOAC handles reservations and arrangements for the transport of pets on Air New Zealand.

AIR RHODESIA (for flights within Rhodesia)

Cabin: If you make reservations a week or so before you wish to travel, small pets may be carried in the cabin. The aircraft's captain and senior traffic officer must give their okay. The pet must of course be in a carrying case.

Kennels: No kennels available.

Shipping Costs: Information unavailable.

Shipping Procedure: Take your pet to the departure area a few hours before flight time.

Insurance: Air Rhodesia does sell insurance covering your pet. You will get all the information by applying directly to the airline.

ALITALIA AIRLINES

Cabin: Pets are permitted in the cabin (assuming you've made proper reservations) if they fit into a container no larger than 16″ x 20″ x 20″.

Kennels: You must get the kennel yourself—they do not sell them.

Shipping Costs: If shipped at the excess-baggage rate (see chapter's introductory remarks for explanation), the tariff is 1% of the normal one-way first-class jet fare per kilo (2.2 pounds). Cargo rates vary with distance. If your pet is flying from New York to Rome the rate is $1.41 per pound.

Shipping Procedure: If you notify Alitalia at least 48 hours before departure, they will guarantee that your pet will be on the same flight.

Insurance: The insurance available through Alitalia costs $2.50 per $100 declared value.

AMERICAN AIRLINES

For full details, see page 76.

AUA AUSTRIAN AIRLINES

Cabin: If your pet weighs less than 10 pounds you can take it with you in the cabin, provided you have reserved space and that it is in a carrying case.

Kennels: No kennels available.

Shipping Costs: If you ship your pet at the excess-baggage rate (see chapter's introductory remarks for explanation), the cost is 1% of the normal one-way first-class jet fare to your destination per kilo (2.2 pounds) of combined pet and kennel weight. If shipped as cargo, the price varies with destination. If you are shipping your pet from Zurich to Vienna the cost will be 24 cents per pound.

Shipping Procedure: If you notify the airline at least 24 hours before departure that you will be taking your pet, they will guarantee that your pet will be aboard the same flight.

Insurance: None available through the airline; you must make your own arrangements.

AVIANCA AIRLINES

Cabin: If your pet is small and you want to take it in the cabin, you must get the approval of the captain of the aircraft before flight time. If he refuses, you may ship it as cargo. (It must, of course, be in a carrying case.)

Kennels: Avianca's cargo department will make arrangements for a kennel if you give them a few days' notice. You have to check with them on size, weight and cost.

Shipping Procedure: Take your pet to the cargo building (if shipping as air cargo) at least 3 hours before take-off. If you are leaving from New York on an early-morning flight, you may take your pet out to the cargo building the night before. The personnel will exercise and feed your pet and board it on the aircraft in the morning.

Insurance: It is available at the rate of 30 cents per $100 declared value.

BRITISH CALEDONIAN AIRWAYS (Merger of BUA and Caledonian)

Cabin: Only puppies and kittens in carrying cases are permitted in the cabin.

Kennels: You must provide your own.

Shipping Costs: There is no charge for the shipment of your pet. It is considered as your baggage allowance. If your baggage comes in over the allotted weight it will go as standby baggage, which means if there is room on the flight your baggage goes, if not you either pay the excess-baggage rate for your luggage or it goes on another flight. The above holds true only on flights from the United States since British Caledonian flies only charter flights from or to the U.S. Flights within Europe or flights from Europe to destinations other than the U.S. have charges for shipping pets. These charges will be found on inquiry abroad.

Shipping Procedure: Take your pet to the departure area 2 hours before take-off.

Insurance: You must make your own arrangements for insurance.

BRITISH OVERSEAS AIRWAYS CORPORATION (BOAC)

Cabin: No pets allowed.

Kennels: No kennels available.

Shipping Costs: If you send your pet as excess baggage (see chapter's introductory remarks for explanation), the rate is 1% of the normal one-way first-class jet fare per kilo (2.2 pounds) of the weight of your pet plus kennel. If sent as cargo, the rates vary with distance. A sample rate is that of New York to London. The cost is $1.21 per pound.

Shipping Procedure: If you're sending your pet at the cargo rate, deliver it to the cargo building at least 4 hours before departure time. It will be on the same plane so long as you have given the airline 3 days' advance notice.

Insurance: The rate for pets going to London or to Europe is $1.50 for every $100 declared value. If your pet is going to another destination, the rate is $2 for every $100 declared value.

BRITISH WEST INDIAN AIRWAYS (BWIA)

Cabin: Pets in containers small enough to fit under your plane seat are accepted in the cabin.

Kennels: Available on request.

Shipping Costs: Any pet traveling BWIA is charged at the excess-baggage rate (see chapter's introductory remarks for explanation), which is 1% of the one-way first-class jet fare to your destination per kilo (2.2 pounds) of weight of your pet plus its kennel.

Shipping Procedure: Take your pet to the departure area a couple of hours before take-off.

Insurance: Available at a cost of $1 for every $100 declared value.

CANADIAN PACIFIC AIR (CPA)

Cabin: No pets allowed.

Kennels: Available in the following sizes:

Size	Small	Large
L x W x H	15" x 21" x 24"	21" x 30" x 26"
Cost	$11.90	$18

Shipping Costs: The price for shipping your pet is a function of the cost of your ticket. It is independent of the size or weight of your pet. If your ticket costs less than $25, the pet is shipped for $8. Between $25 and $50, pets are shipped for $10. Between $50 and $120, your pet's fare is $12. These rates apply for flights within Canada.

Shipping Procedure: You must check with the agents at the various Canadian airports.

Insurance: Must be arranged by you—the airline does not sell it.

CHINA AIRLINES

Cabin: No pets allowed.

Kennels: They have them for sale. For details contact the airline.

Shipping Costs: Rates vary with distance traveled. The rate from San Francisco to Taipei is $2.12 per pound.

Shipping Procedure: Take your pet to the cargo building 3 hours before departure.

Insurance: Available at 5% of the cargo charge with a $5 minimum.

EASTERN AIRLINES

For full details, see page 80.

EL AL ISRAEL AIRLINES

Cabin: If your pet in its kennel weighs less than 10 pounds you can take it in the cabin.

Kennels: None available.

Shipping Costs: If you're sending your pet at the excess-baggage rate (see chapter's introductory remarks for explanation), it will cost you $3.66 per pound. If you are shipping it as air cargo, the charge is $1.60 per pound.

Shipping Procedure: Pets shipped as cargo should be taken to the cargo building at least 3 hours before departure.

Insurance: You must make your own provisions—El Al does not carry pet insurance.

FINNAIR

Cabin: No pets allowed.

Kennels: The sizes, weights and prices of Finnair kennels are listed below. (For explanation of pound weight versus volume weight see chapter's introductory remarks.)

Type	#1	#2	#3	#4
L x W	11" x 14"	16" x 19"	20" x 24"	20" x 30"
x H	x 19"	x 24"	x 30"	x 36"
Pound Weight	5 lbs.	9 lbs.	16 lbs.	18 lbs.
Volume Weight	14 lbs.	38 lbs.	74 lbs.	111 lbs.
Cost	$9.45	$14.70	$21	$23

Shipping Costs: If shipped as excess baggage (see chapter's introductory remarks for explanation), the rate is 1% of the normal one-way first-class jet fare to your destination per kilo (2.2 pounds) of weight of your pet plus its kennel. Cargo rates vary with distance.

Shipping Procedure: Your pet should be taken to the cargo building at least 3 hours before flight time. If you do this, they will guarantee that your pet will be aboard the same plane.

Insurance: Finnair will sell you insurance at the rate of $5 per $100 declared value of your pet.

GARUDA INDONESIAN AIRWAYS

Cabin: Small pets in carrying cases are permitted in the cabin.

Kennels: None available.

Shipping Costs and Procedures: Garuda suggests that reservations be made and confirmed well in advance of departure if you are taking your pet. Prices and procedures vary with destination. You must check with them directly.

Insurance: You must make outside arrangements because Garuda does not sell insurance for pets.

HONDURAS AIRLINES (SAHSA)

Cabin: No pets allowed.

Kennels: None available.

Shipping Costs: Shipping your pet as cargo costs 150% of the air-freight charge.

Shipping Procedure: Your pet should be taken to the cargo department 5 hours before flight time.

Insurance: None available through the airline.

IBERIA AIRLINES

Cabin: Iberia permits one dog or cat in first class and one in economy class provided the pet (with kennel) weighs less than 9 pounds.

Kennels: None available.

Shipping Costs: If you're sending your pet at the excess-baggage rate (see chapter's introductory remarks for explanation), it will cost you a little more than $4 per pound. If sent as cargo, the rate varies with distance. From New York to Madrid your pet will cost $1.29 per pound of pet plus kennel.

Shipping Procedure: Make your reservations as early as you can. On the day of departure, take your pet to the cargo building at least 4 hours before flight time.

Insurance: Iberia does not sell pet insurance.

IRISH INTERNATIONAL AIRLINES (*Aer Lingus*)

Cabin: No pets allowed in cabins, except, of course, Seeing Eye dogs.

Kennels: None available.

Shipping Costs: If your pet is being shipped as cargo, the rate is a function of the distance traveled. As an example, the rate from New York to Dublin is $1.17 per pound (pet plus kennel).

Shipping Procedure: If you reserve space a few days in advance of your flight, Irish International will make every attempt to get your pet on the same plane.

Insurance: The insurance rate is $1.50 per $100 declared value.

JAPAN AIR LINES

Cabin: Small pets in carrying cases are permitted in the cabin.

Kennels: The following kennels are sold by Japan Air Lines:

Type	Small	Medium	Large	Extra-large
L x W	16" x 12"	24" x 14"	30" x 18"	40" x 23"
x H	x 12"	x 16"	x 24"	x 27"
Cost	$6	$8	$10	$15

Shipping Costs: The excess-baggage rate (see chapter's introductory remarks for explanation), is 1% of the one-way first-class jet fare per kilo (2.2 pounds) of combined pet and kennel weight. The cargo rate varies with weight and distance to destination. If, for example, you're flying from New York to Tokyo and your pet plus its kennel weighs less than 100 pounds, the cost is $2.15 per pound. If your pet in its kennel weighs more than 100 pounds, the cost is $1.60 per pound.

Shipping Procedure: If shipping your pet via cargo, deliver it to the cargo building at least 3 hours before flight time.

Insurance: Insurance is available at a rate of $5 per $100 declared value.

KLM ROYAL DUTCH AIRLINES

Cabin: Pets are permitted in the cabin if the carrying case they occupy is no larger than 12″ x 16″ x 16″. The weight of the animal plus container must be less than 17.6 pounds.

Kennels: Containers for cabin-size pets are sold at KLM offices for $2. The following kennels for cargo shipment are for sale:

Type	Small	Medium	Large	Extra-large
L x W x H	19″ x 12″ x 14″	24″ x 16″ x 19″	30″ x 20″ x 24″	36″ x 20″ x 30″
Pound Weight	5 lbs.	9 lbs.	16 lbs.	18 lbs.
Volume Weight	14 lbs.	38 lbs.	74 lbs.	111 lbs.
Cost	$9	$14	$20	$22

Shipping Costs: If sent as excess baggage (see chapter's introductory remarks for explanation), the rate is 1% of the one-way first-class jet fare to your destination per kilo (2.2 pounds) of the weight of your pet plus its kennel. Cargo rates vary with size and distance to your destination. If your pet is flying from New York to Amsterdam the rate is $1.29 per pound of pet plus kennel.

Shipping Procedure: To be sure that your pet will be aboard your plane, notify the cargo department of KLM at least 3 days before departure. On the day of your flight take your pet to the cargo building at least 3 hours before flight time.

Insurance: For pets traveling within North America and Europe, insurance is available at the rate of $1.50 per $100 declared value. If your pet is traveling to another destination you must arrange the insurance on your own.

LAN–CHILEAN INTERNATIONAL AIRLINE

Cabin: No pets allowed.

Kennels: None available through Lan–Chilean.

Shipping Costs: If shipped as excess baggage (see chapter's introductory remarks for explanation), the cost is 1% of the normal one-way first-class jet fare to your destination per kilo (2.2 pounds) of combined animal and kennel weight. If shipped as cargo, the price varies with destination. From New York to Santiago the cost would be $1.59 per pound (animal plus kennel).

Shipping Procedure: Notify the airline at least 1½ weeks before your planned departure that you will be taking your pet along. Deliver your pet to the cargo building at least 5 hours before departure.

Insurance: None available through the airline.

LOT POLISH AIRLINES

Cabin: No pets allowed.

Kennels: Lot sells kennels for large pets. For sizes and costs you will have to contact them directly. They recommend that if you are shipping a small pet, you provide your own kennel.

Shipping Costs: Information available through the airline.

Shipping Procedure: They will make no advance booking arrangements for your pet. You are advised to take your pet to the airport 2 hours before flight time. If there is too much cargo on the plane, they will care for your pet until the next flight out and ship it then.

Insurance: None available through the airline.

LUFTHANSA–GERMAN AIRLINES

Cabin: No pets allowed.

Kennels: Lufthansa has the following kennels for sale. The prices quoted are for pets of Lufthansa passengers. Kennels will cost more if you buy them but travel another airline.

Type	1	1a	2	2a	3	4	4a	5
L x W x H	17″ x 13″ x 14″	18″ x 10″ x 12″	22″ x 17″ x 19″	22″ x 17″ x 15″	29″ x 20″ x 26″	37″ x 24″ x 30″	35″ x 20″ x 28″	43″ x 28″ x 35″
Pound Weight	5 lbs.	4 lbs.	11 lbs.	9 lbs.	18 lbs.	30 lbs.	28 lbs.	44 lbs.
Volume Weight	16 lbs.	11 lbs.	37 lbs.	29 lbs.	78 lbs.	137 lbs.	101 lbs.	217 lbs.
Cost	$6	$2.25	$8.50	$7.25	$11	$18.25	$16.60	25.50

Shipping Costs: If your pet is shipped at the excess-baggage rate (see chapter's introductory remarks for explanation), the cost is 1% of the one-way first-class jet fare to your destination per kilo (2.2 pounds) of the weight of your pet plus its kennel. If sent as cargo, the rate varies with distance. From New York to Frankfort your pet plus its kennel will cost $1.38 per pound.

Shipping Procedure: Take your pet to the cargo building 3 hours before flight time if you are shipping it as air cargo. If you are shipping it as excess baggage, take it with you to the departure terminal about a half hour before check-in time.

NEW ZEALAND NATIONAL AIRWAYS CORPORATION—See British Overseas Airways Corporation

BOAC handles the booking in the United States for New Zealand National Airways.

NORTHEAST AIRLINES

For full details, see page 83.

NORTHWEST ORIENT AIRLINES

For full details, see page 84.

PAN AMERICAN AIRWAYS

Cabin: Small pets in carrying cases are permitted.
Kennels: The following molded-plastic kennels are available:

Type	Toy	Small	Medium	Large
L x W	19" x 12"	22" x 17"	31" x 19"	38" x 20"
x H	x 15"	x 17"	x 22"	x 26"
Pound Weight	6 lbs.	9 lbs.	16 lbs.	21 lbs.
Volume Weight	28 lbs.	49 lbs.	97 lbs.	137 lbs.
Cost	$10.50	$12.50	$21.50	$26.50

Shipping Costs: The excess-baggage rate (see chapter's introductory remarks for explanation), is 1% of the one-way first-class jet fare to your destination per kilo (2.2 pounds) of combined pet and kennel weight. Cargo charges vary with the destination.

Shipping Procedure: Deliver your pet to the cargo building 4 hours before flight time if it is being sent as cargo. If your pet is being shipped as excess baggage, you can take it with you to the departure terminal 1 hour before flight time.

Insurance: Insurance is available at the rate of $1 per $100 declared value. There is a minimum charge of $5.

SABENA BELGIAN WORLD AIRLINES

Cabin: Small pets are allowed.

Kennels: Notify a Sabena office at least 4 days before departure if you wish to buy a kennel from them. They have 4 sizes, ranging in price from $7 to $12. If you have need of a special kennel, give them a week's notice so that they will have it on hand.

Shipping Costs: Excess-baggage costs (see chapter's introductory remarks for explanation) are figured at 1% of the one-way first-class jet fare per kilo (2.2 pounds) of combined pet and kennel weight. Cargo charges depend on the distance to your destination. From New York to Brussels the rate is $1.29 per pound of pet plus kennel.

Shipping Procedure: If you are shipping your pet at the excess-baggage rate, take it to the departure terminal 2 hours before take-off. If shipping a pet as cargo, it should be at the cargo building 3 hours before flight time.

Insurance: Insurance is available at the rate of $1.50 per $100 declared value.

SCANDINAVIAN AIRLINES (SAS)

Cabin: No pets allowed.

Kennels: SAS sells the following kennels:

Type	Small	Medium	Large
L x W x H	18″ x 12″ x 16″	24″ x 14″ x 20″	36″ x 20″ x 26″
Pound Weight	9 lbs.	15 lbs.	25 lbs.
Volume Weight	18 lbs.	34 lbs.	93 lbs.
Cost	$10	$13	$17

Shipping Costs: If shipped as excess baggage (see chapter's introductory remarks for explanation), your pet's fare will be 1% of the normal one-way first-class jet fare to your destination. Cargo charges are based on the distance traveled.

Shipping Procedure: If shipping your pet at the excess-baggage rate, go with it to the departure terminal a half hour before regular check-in time. If shipped as cargo, take it to the cargo building at least 4 hours before flight time. If you do this, SAS will guarantee that your animal will be on the same flight.

Insurance: If your pet is flying between New York and Scandinavia, the rate is 30 cents per $100 declared value. There is a minimum of $1.

SWISSAIR

Cabin: Small pets are allowed in the cabin.

Kennels: A list of kennels available through Swissair follows. Prices quoted in dollars indicate kennels available in New York. The prices quoted in Swiss francs are for kennels sold in Europe.

Type		
Galvanized Wire		
L x W x H	24″ x 15″ x 21″	36″ x 21″ x 30″
Pound Weight	18 lbs.	34 lbs.
Volume Weight	40 lbs.	117 lbs.
Cost	$11.50	$16
Wood Size in centimeters		
L x W x H	55 x 25 x 40	70 x 45 x 55	104 x 52 x 65
Weight	4 kilos	9 kilos	14 kilos
Cost	Fr. 25	Fr. 35	Fr. 45

Aluminum*
Size in centimeters

L x W x H	72 x 45 x 51	97 x 58 x 68
Weight	9 kilos	15 kilos
Cost	Fr. 25	Fr. 35

Kennels for pets carried in the cabin are available in 2 sizes. The smaller one costs $1 and the larger $1.50.

Shipping Costs: Pets shipped at the excess-baggage rate (see chapter's introductory remarks for explanation) cost 1% of the one-way first-class jet fare to your destination. Pets shipped as cargo are charged a rate that varies with the distance traveled. The rate on a flight from New York to Zurich is $1.38 per pound of pet plus kennel.

Shipping Procedure: Notify the cargo department at least 5 days before departure if you're shipping your pet as cargo. On the day of your flight, take your pet to the cargo department at least 3 hours before take-off. If this is done, they say that your pet stands a 99% chance of being aboard the same flight. If for some reason your pet is not on the same flight, they will care for it until they board it on the very next flight.

Insurance: Pets are automatically covered by the same insurance that covers your baggage. That is $16.50 for every 2.2 pounds your pet weighs. If you want additional insurance you have to arrange that privately.

TAP PORTUGUESE AIRWAYS

Cabin: No pets allowed.
Kennels: TAP sells the following kennels:
   Small—$15
   Medium—$20
   Large—$25
The size and weight of the kennels can be found by inquiry at a TAP office.

* The aluminum kennels are available on a rental basis only.

Shipping Costs: If you're shipping your pet at the excess-baggage rate (see chapter's introductory remarks for explanation), it will cost you 1% of the normal one-way first-class jet fare per kilo (2.2 pounds) of combined pet and kennel weight. Cargo charges vary with distance.

Shipping Procedure: If you are shipping your pet as cargo, deliver it to the airline at least 3½ hours before take-off.

Insurance: Insurance is available. The rates depend on the distance your pet is traveling.

TRANS-AUSTRALIA AIRLINES (TAA)

Cabin: Only Seeing Eye dogs are permitted in the cabin.

Kennels: Pet packs (for puppies and kittens) are sold for $1.50 (Australian dollars). Wire-mesh kennels are available on a rental basis at a charge of $2 regardless of size. They come in a range of heights from 14″ to 25″ and in length from 18″ to 33″. All dogs must be muzzled before being put into a kennel.

Shipping Costs: You can use your free-baggage allowance for transport of your pet.

Shipping Procedure: Take this one up with the appropriate personnel in Australia.

Insurance: Pets are automatically insured at the same liability rate as your baggage. Additional insurance must be arranged privately.

TRANS WORLD AIRLINES (TWA)

For full details, see page 90.

Services and regulations are the same as on domestic flights. For cargo rates to your destination, check with the airline.

VARIG AIRLINES

Cabin: Varig permits 1 pet per flight in the cabin, but only if you are traveling first class.

Kennels: None available.

Shipping Costs: The cargo rate for shipping your pet varies with distance. If your pet is flying from New York to Caracas, the rate is $4.79 per kilo (2.2 pounds) of combined pet plus kennel weight.

Shipping Procedure: Take your pet to the departure terminal 1½ hours before flight time.

Insurance: Not available.

The following airlines carry pets as cargo but do not carry them in cabins:

Aerlinte Eireann
Aerolineas Peruanas S.A.
Air Ceylon
Air Guinee
Air Vietnam
Alia—The Royal Jordanian Airlines
Ansett—ANA Airline of Australia
Cyprus Airways Limited
Direccao de Exploracao dos Transported Aereos (DTA)
Empress Consolidada Cubana de Aviacion
Ethiopian Airlines S.C.
Flying Tiger Line
Kingdom of Libya Airlines
Kuwait Airways
Linea Aerea del Cobre Ltd.
Malta Airlines
Philippine Air Lines
Qantas Airways
Servicos Aereos Cruzeiro Do Sul S.A.
Suidwes Lugdiens (Eiendoms) Beperk
Trans-Mediterranean Airways
United Arab Airlines
Venezuelan International Airways (VIASA)

These airlines will accept pets both as cargo and in the cabin:

Air Malawi Ltd.
East African Airways
Saudi Arabian Airlines
Union de Transports Aeriens

BY SHIP

As you will see below, many ship lines take pets. The cost of shipment is a bit simpler than on planes because it is independent of the size of your pet or its weight. Only difference in species accounts for the differences in rates. Those lines having kennels have attendants who will take care to feed and exercise your pet (unless otherwise noted). Remember to have all necessary health documents and import papers for your pet before you board the ship—and *bon voyage*.

CUNARD LINE

Pets are carried on all transatlantic crossings but *not* on cruises. Kennels are provided for dogs and you should reserve one as early as you can since their number is limited. Cats should be taken on board in their own baskets or carrying cases.

Shipping Costs: These prices are for eastbound crossings. When traveling westbound you will have to pay in British currency. Dogs are charged $50, cats $10, birds (1 or 2 per cage) $5, and birds (more than 2 per cage) $10.

Regulations: Pets are forbidden to enter passenger cabins or areas of the ship designated solely for use by passengers.

FRENCH LINE

Having crossed from France to New York with Louie on the S.S. *France,* I (Paula) can give you firsthand information about this ship. The kennel area of the *France* is quite spacious and has cages large enough for a Great Dane. In fact, on our crossing, one kennel was housing a *pair* of Great Danes. The exterior area of the kennel is equipped with large enclosed pens so that animals can be out in the fresh sea air in good weather. There are even fire hydrants, a lamppost and stone markers. The man in charge of caring for the pets was very kind. Pets were taken for frequent walks and passengers with pets can walk them in the outside area of the kennel at any time they wish. The interior section of the kennel is open from about 6 A.M. to 9 P.M. Pets are fed anything that you request and on several evenings they dined on very fine looking steak and roast beef.

Shipping Costs: Dogs cost $50 per crossing, cats $10. Kennels are provided for both.

Regulations: The formal regulations of the French Line state that your pet must be kept in the kennel. However, if you have a cabin to yourself, you may request permission from the purser to keep your pet with you. Such permission is granted with the proviso that people staying in adjoining cabins are not disturbed by your pet. Of course, if your pet makes a mess of the cabin you will be asked to return it to the kennel. All pets must stay in the kennel area during the stop at Southampton (unless they are getting on or off the ship). If you are keeping your pet in your cabin you can make arrangements with the kennel attendant for feeding. I took Louie to the kennel for his dinner and to be exercised. I also took him there several times a day for the obvious reason that that is the one place where it was possible for him to get fresh air, a run and where he was permitted to "relieve" himself. Pets are allowed on most French Line cruises.

GDYNIA AMERICA LINE (POLISH OCEAN LINES)

Shipping Costs: The rate for dogs is $50 per crossing, for cats it's $10, birds (1 or 2 per cage) cost $5, and cases containing more than 2 birds cost $10.

Greek Line

All the Greek Line ships have kennel facilities for dogs of all sizes, and for cats and birds. The kennel steward handles the care and feeding of the pets and he sets the times when you can visit with them.

Shipping Costs: Dogs are charged $50 per crossing, cats cost $10, and birds (1 or 2 per cage) are $5. If there are 3 to 5 birds per cage, the cost is $10; and if there are more than 5 birds in a cage, the cost is $2 per bird.

Italian Line

Pets are carried on all transatlantic voyages but *not* on cruises.

Shipping Costs: Dogs are charged $50 per crossing, cats $10.

Regulations: Pets are permitted only in the designated kennel area.

Ivaran Lines

Since the freighters of this line have no special kennel facilities you must keep your pet with you in your cabin. You must also arrange the feeding of your pet yourself, either by bringing all necessary food aboard with you or making prior arrangements with the line.

Shipping Costs: The charge for carrying dogs is $40, cats cost $15, and birds are $7.50 if there are 1 or 2 in a cage.

Moore-McCormack Lines

These ships do not have kennels so you have to provide your own. You must also make your own arrangements for the feeding of your pet.

Shipping Costs: Dogs and cats are carried at the rate of $10 per day.

Regulations: You cannot take your pet out of the area designated as kennel facility.

NEDLLOYD LINES

You must supply your own kennel or crate for your pet. The ship's personnel will feed your pet.

Shipping Costs: The charge for any animal carried is $20. This goes for a cage of birds as well.

Regulations: Pets must be kept in the area selected for them. They are not allowed in your cabin. The personnel of each ship decides what the visiting hours are.

NORTH GERMAN LLOYD

Kennels are provided for pets. The ones for dogs measure 3' x 3' x 4'. Cat kennels are 2' x 2' x 3'. If your pet requires a larger kennel notify the line well before sailing. Pets are fed in the morning. Their meal consists of cooked beef with rice. If you want your pet to be fed canned food you must bring it along and make arrangements with the kennel personnel.

Shipping Costs: The fare for dogs is $50, for cats $15. Bird cages holding 1 or 2 birds cost $5, if there are 3 or more birds the price is $10.

Regulations: You may visit your pet as often as you'd like for as long as you'd like but you cannot take it out of the kennel area.

PACIFIC FAR EAST LINE

When traveling with a pet on this line, you must provide the kennel or cage. You must also arrange with the steward to care for your pet. The kennels or crates are stowed on the deck in an area deemed appropriate by the master or chief officer. Cats may be kept in your cabin if you are the only occupant(s), assuming that your cat is used to staying indoors and you so desire it.

Shipping Costs: If you are traveling with a dog there is a charge of $100 for each dog. The fare for cats is $15, and for birds (if there are 1 or 2 in a cage) the fare is $7.50. In addition to these charges you must remember that you have to pay for acquisition of a kennel or crate and also pay for the attendance of a steward.

NOTE: Before you may board ship with your dog, you must obtain a certificate stating that your dog has been inoculated against hydrophobia.

SWEDISH AMERICAN LINE

Pets are carried only on transatlantic crossings, *not* on cruises. The kennels have doors, windows, lighting and electric radiators. There are special attendants to care for your pets.

Shipping Costs: The fare for a dog is $50, for a cat $10.

WHAT'S IT LIKE IN . . . ?

All right, so getting there is half the fun. But, then what? Will you arrive on a foreign shore only to find hotel doors slammed in your pet's face? Will you have to trudge the weary length of a strange city because public transport won't let you aboard with your animal? What if you run out of flea powder or your pet breaks its leash . . . can you find replacements? Are there grooming services to wash away the grime of travel? Is there a veterinarian in the place should your pet feel faint? And, most importantly, do they sell pet food or must you use up your baggage allowance on Ken-L Ration?

In this chapter we try to answer these questions so vital to your own and your pet's traveling pleasure. Neither our time nor our budget was sufficiently extensive to cover the entire globe. We have confined ourselves to those countries that are most popular with travelers and, as we've mentioned before, we'd be delighted to hear of your own experiences in any country.

Two general recommendations we'd like to make before you set forth: Never hesitate to ask for help from the people at your hotel or at tourist offices. Not only are they extremely helpful, as a rule, but we've found that people are especially responsive if there's an animal involved. And don't be afraid of foreign telephones. Telephone companies in many countries offer all manner of marvelous services from sight-seeing advice and morning wake-up calls to making your train reservations for you. These courtesies greatly simplify your life. And that means that you are more relaxed, your pet is more relaxed, and you both have that much more time to enjoy exploring a new country.

ARGENTINA

The principal cities in Argentina are well supplied with dog food, pet shops and veterinarians. Most of the large hotels do accept pets but it's a good idea to request permission in advance. That holds true no matter what type of accommodations you're seeking.

Pets are allowed on public transport only if they are in a carrier. The railroads permit pets in baggage cars only. They must be in a sturdy container, accompanied by their health certificates.

Outdoor cafés and most restaurants have no objections to well-behaved animals, so your pet may enjoy a great deal of Argentine social life with you.

AUSTRIA

Austria is one of those curious countries in which people are extremely fond of pets and *yet* you may run into a problem finding a hotel that will accept you with your animal. Personally, I (Geraldine) had no difficulty in Vienna but other people report that they did, so it seems better to check with your travel agent or the local tourist office in advance.

Pets are permitted on all public transportation but they

should either be muzzled or you should carry a muzzle with you in case someone insists your dog wear it.

You have to keep your pet leashed in the carefully tended city parks but it may run free in more casual parks, such as the Vienna Woods.

It's rare that a restaurant will not allow you in with your pet. Mrs. Dorothy Servos of the Canadian Travel Bureau lived in Austria for three years and she painted a charming picture of Vienna at teatime. Cafés and teashops are very popular and late every afternoon they are crowded with people, each of whom has brought his dog, which is resting quietly under the table while its owner unwinds after a weary day. If you are planning on trying one of the more elegant restaurants, we suggest you check with them in advance in case they are the exception to the rule.

There are many excellent veterinarians available in Austria and you will have no trouble finding grooming services or pet shops either. Prepared pet food may not be so readily found. Since most Austrians buy fresh meat for their animals, you may have to switch from canned to fresh food while staying there.

BERMUDA

You can fly off to Bermuda with an untroubled mind if your pet is a small or medium-sized animal. Both of you are welcome to relax on the beach at the hotels and guesthouses listed below. Pets are not allowed in dining areas and restaurants. If you're reluctant to leave your pet alone while you have an evening out, you can make arrangements for a "pet sitter" through your hotel or an employment bureau. The rates are pretty much the same as for baby-sitters.

There are four veterinarians practicing in Bermuda and you'll find them listed in the telephone directory. Each has facilities for treating and boarding animals. The island also has several pet shops; two that sell supplies are Purina Store and Pic-A-Pet. You can find prepared pet food at all food stores and supermarkets. Some fresh meat is available, such as ox cheeks, shavings and liver. There is no fresh horsemeat so be prepared to make substitutions if that's been the mainstay of your animal's diet.

If you are planning to stay in Bermuda any length of time, you should have your dog licensed as soon as its Department of Agriculture permit expires. Dog registration is handled by the Bermuda Post Office at the following rates: females, $4.80; spayed females, $2.40; and males, $2.40.

As to transportation, taxi and bus drivers have the option to refuse to carry any animal that might disturb other passengers or scratch up the seats. They generally permit small animals, carried by hand or in a case, and Seeing Eye dogs are always allowed.

On the whole, guesthouse and hotel proprietors prefer small, well-behaved animals and permission must always be requested in advance. Animals must be leashed while on actual hotel grounds, but you may take your pet for a swim and allow it to run loose on the beach provided it doesn't kick sand on everyone else. Some hotels will also feed your pet so be sure to ask the management about this. For those of you with larger pets, contact Inverurie Hotel, whose management is exceptionally fond of animals. They accept all size dogs during dog shows and, if your dog is well behaved, at other times as well. They will also feed your pet. And now to the hotels and guesthouses that welcome pets.

The Anchorage
Archlyn Villa
Ashley Hall
Belmont Hotel
Blue Sea Cottage
The Breakers Club

Breezie Brae
Capistrano/Harringay
Castle Harbour
Deepdene Manor
Elbow Beach
   (Cottages only)

Fourways Inn
Gables Guest House
Grape Bay Cottages
Highlands
Inverurie Hotel
La Cabane
Marley Beach
Middleton Cottages
Montgomery Cottages
Myrtlebank
Pillar Ville
Pomander Gate
Princess Hotel

Que Sera
The Reefs
Rick-A-Tan
St. George Hotel
Salt Kettle
    (Cottages only)
Sea Horse Cottages
Seamont Guest House
Sonesta Beach
Sugar Cane Hotel
Teucer Place
Valley Cottages
White Heron

BRAZIL

From a pet owner's viewpoint, it seems easier to live in Brazil than to visit there. They have a very active Sociedad Protectore de Animals, their equivalent of our A.S.P.C.A., and veterinarians, grooming services, pet shops and pet food are readily found. However, most hotels do not accept pets, although you should check this again with your travel agent. As to public transport, the only response we've gotten to our research is that pets are permitted to travel in private cars and taxis. If your pet is small enough to be carried in a case, we suggest you at least give the public transportation facilities a whirl, as it seems inconceivable they'd refuse a pet that is so obviously not a nuisance.

CANADA

Traveling with a pet in Canada is often even easier than in the United States. Once you've satisfied the entry require-

ments (see page 124), you can take your pet with you practically everywhere. Your animal may travel, uncaged and/or
unmuzzled, on all public transport within the cities. Intercity bus lines, such as Gray Coach and Voyager, will let you
take your pet if it's in a carrier. Trains permit animals in the
baggage cars only, except for Seeing Eye dogs, which are
allowed to accompany their owners in both coach and private
compartments. You may visit your pet en route to feed and
exercise it or you can arrange with the trainmen to do so.
They are generally very kind and quite willing to look after
any animal if it's friendly to strangers. Water is available in
the baggage cars but you have to provide the bowls for it
and for your pet's food. Generally speaking, your pet should
travel in a crate or kennel that you provide. Dogs may be un-
crated if they are outfitted with a securely fitting collar or
harness with a chain or leash, and a muzzle. The rate for
train transportation of pets is quite low and is based on the
mileage involved. Pets traveling in a kennel cost less than if
on a leash. For example, a dog weighing up to 100 pounds
will cost $16 on a leash or $8 in a kennel to travel from Montreal to Winnipeg.

The situation regarding pets in eating establishments is
quite mixed. There are no federal statutes against an animal
accompanying you to a restaurant so it's really up to the individual restaurateur. The very fanciest restaurants usually
don't permit pets, but a great many other restaurants do. If
they prefer that your pet stay out of the actual dining area,
they'll arrange a spot for it to wait in. You can always ask
the advice of personnel at your hotel as to which restaurants
in the area accept pets. If there are none or if you prefer to
eat at one that forbids animals, your hotel or motel manager
will generally make arrangements for someone to look after
your pet while you are out. Should you be traveling in the
winter months in the colder sections of Canada, then even
those dining places that normally do not permit pets will

allow your animal to come in out of the bitter cold and will give it something warm to drink.

Canada is very similar to the United States in that pet food, pet shops, veterinarians and grooming services are available everywhere. Again, as in our own country, pets are permitted in all Canadian national parks if they're on a leash of some sort.

As to hotels and motels, you'll have no trouble finding one that will accept your pet. We can offer no hard-and-fast ruling on this because it *is* the individual proprietor's decision but the following list of places that definitely welcome pets should reassure you that you may travel anywhere in Canada and find lodgings for your entire entourage.

Single = S   Double = D

Alberta

CALGARY

Calgary Inn. 4th Ave. at 3rd St. S.W. Tel.: (403) 266-1611. S $18–; D $22–.

Highlander Motor Hotel. On Trans-Canada Hwy., 1818 16th Ave. N.W. Tel.: (403) 289-1965. S $12–; D $15.50–.

Holiday Inn. 8th Ave. at 6th St. S.W. Tel.: (403) 263-7600. S $15.50–; D $19.50–.

EDMONTON

Holiday Inn. 107th St. & 100th Ave. Tel.: (403) 429-2861. S $17.50–; D $22–.

British Columbia

FAIRMONT

Fairmont Hot Springs Resort. On Hwy. 95. Box. No. 1. Tel.: (604) 342-9225. S $12–; D $16–.

Make some special plans for him too!

Vancouver

Bayshore Inn. W. Georgia at Cardero St. Tel.: (604) 682-3377. S $18–; D $23–.

Georgia. Georgia at Howe. Tel.: (604) 682-5566. S $16.50–; D $20–.

Holiday Inn. 1110 Howe St. at Helmcken. Tel.: (604) 684-2151. S $15.50–; D $19–.

Victoria

Imperial Inn. Discovery at Douglas. Tel.: (604) 382-2111. S $19–; D $24–.

Red Lion Motor Inn. On Hwy. 1 at 3366 Douglas St. Tel.: (604) 385-3366. S $12–; D $15–.

Manitoba

Winnipeg

Ramada Inn. 1824 Pembina Hwy. Tel.: (204) 452-5543. S $14.50–; D $18–.

Sheraton-Carlton Motor Hotel. Carlton St. & St. Mary Ave. Tel.: (204) 942-0881. S $12–; D $16–.

Winnipeg Inn. 2 Lombard Pl. Tel.: (204) 957-1350. S $17–; D $22–.

New Brunswick

Saint John

Holiday Inn. Waterloo & Crown Sts. Tel.: (506) 657-3610. S $12–; D $16–.

Newfoundland

Clarenville

Holiday Inn. Trans-Canada Hwy. Tel.: (709) 466-7911. S $11; D $16–.

CORNER BROOK

Holiday Inn. West St. at Tod St. Tel.: (709) 634-5381. S $12–; D $17–.

GANDER

Holiday Inn. Trans-Canada Hwy. at Caldwell St. Tel.: (709) 256-3981. S $12–; D $17–.

ST. JOHN'S

Holiday Inn. Portugal Cove Rd. at Confederation Dr. Start of Trans-Canada Hwy. Tel.: (709) 722-0506. S $15–; D $19–.

Nova Scotia

HALIFAX-DARTMOUTH

Holiday Inn. Wyse Rd., Dartmouth. Tel.: (902) 463-1100. S $12–; D $16–.

SYDNEY

Holiday Inn. Hwy. # 4 King's Rd. Tel.: (902) 539-6750. S $13–; D $18.50–.

Ontario

BARRIE

Holiday Inn. Hwys. 400 & 27, Essa Rd. exit. Tel.: (705) 728-6191. S $15; D $19.50–.

BRANTFORD

Holiday Inn. Hwy. 403 & Park Rd. Tel.: (519) 753-8651. S $15; D $19.50–.

CHATHAM

Holiday Inn. 25 Keil Dr. N. & Grand Ave. (Hwy. 2). Tel.: (519) 354-5030. S $15; D $20–.

FORT WILLIAM-PORT ARTHUR

Holiday Inn. Donald & Brodie Sts. Tel.: (807) 623-1581. S $15; D $20–.

HAMILTON

Holiday Inn. 150 King St. E. at Catharine. Tel.: (416) 528-3451. S $17.50–; D $21.50–.
Sheraton-Connaught Hotel & Motor Inn. 112 King St. E. Tel.: (416) 527-5071. S $12–; D $16–.

HESPELER-GALT

Holiday Inn. Hwys. 401 & 24 at Exit 36 off Hwy. 401. Tel.: (519) 658-4601. S $15.50–; D $20–.

HUNTSVILLE-HIDDEN VALLEY

Holiday Inn. Hwy. 60, 5 mi. east of Huntsville. Tel.: (705) 789-2301. S $15; D. $19.50.

KENORA

Holiday Inn. Trans-Canada Hwy. #17 on Lake of the Woods. Tel.: (807) 468-5521. S $14–; D $19–.

KINGSTON

Holiday Inn. End of Princess St. on Lake Ontario. Tel.: (613) 542-7311. S $16–; D $23–.

KITCHENER-WATERLOO

Holiday Inn. 30 Fairway Ave. at Hwy. 8. Exit 35 off Hwy. 401. Tel.: (519) 744-6341. S $15–; D $19.50–.

LONDON

Holiday Inn. 1210 Wellington Rd., north of Hwy. 401. Exit 20. Tel.: (519) 433-0121. S $16–; D $19.50–.

Holiday Inn. 299 King St. Tel.: (519) 433-1271. S $17.50–; D $21.50–.

OAKVILLE

Holiday Inn. Queen Elizabeth Hwy. at Trafalgar Rd. exit. Tel.: (416) 845-7561. S $16–; D $20.50–.

NIAGARA FALLS

Park Motor Hotel. On Ontario 3A & 20. Clifton Hill. Tel.: (416) 358-3293. S $16–; D $18–.

Sheraton-Brock Hotel & Motor Inn. 5685 Falls Ave. Tel.: (416) 354-7441. S $12.50–; D $18.50–.

OSHAWA

Holiday Inn. On Hwy. 401 at Exit 72. Tel.: (416) 576-5101. S $17–; D $21–.

OTTAWA

Holiday Inn. 350 Dalhousie St. Tel.: (613) 236-0201. S $18.50–; D $21.50–.

PETERBOROUGH

Holiday Inn. 150 George St. Tel.: (705) 743-1144. S $15–; D $20.50–.

ST. CATHARINES

Holiday Inn. Jct. of Queen Elizabeth Hwy. & Lake St. Tel.: (416) 934-2561. S $14–; D $19.50–.

SARNIA

Holiday Inn. Hwy. 40, Point Edward. Tel.: (519) 336-4680. S $16.50–; D $20.50–.

SAULT STE. MARIE

Sheraton-Caswell Motor Inn. 503 Trunk Rd. (Hwy. 17 E.). Tel.: (705) 253-2327. S $11.50–; D $16–.

SUDBURY

Holiday Inn. Ring Rd. at Notre Dame Ave. Tel.: (705) 675-1123. S $17.50–; D $22.50–.

TORONTO

Holiday Inn—Don Valley. Don Valley Pkwy. & Eglinton Ave. E. on Wynford Dr. Expswy. Tel.: (416) 449-4111. S $21.50–; D $26–.

Holiday Inn—East. Hwy. 401 & Warden Ave. Scarborough. Tel.: (416) 293-8171. S $19–; D $23–.

Holiday Inn—Etobicoke. Hwy. 27 bet. Hwy. 401 & Queen Elizabeth. Tel.: (416) 621-2121. S $19–; D $23–.

Holiday Inn—Malton Int'l. 970 Dixon Rd. Rexdale 605. Tel.: (416) 677-7611. S $20.50–; D $25–.

Holiday Inn—Yorkdale. On Hwy. 401 at Dufferin Rd. Tel.: (416) 789-5161. S $20–; D $28–.

King Edward-Sheraton Hotel. 37 King St. E. Tel.: (416) 368-7474. S $12–; D $20–.

WINDSOR

Holiday Inn. 480 Riverside Dr. W. Tel.: (519) 253-4411. S $17.50–; D $22.50–.

Sheraton-Viscount Motor Hotel. 1150 Ouellette Ave. Tel.: (519) 252-2741. S $12.50–; D $15.50–.

Quebec

MONTREAL

Holiday Inn—Chauteaubriand. 6500 Cote de Liesse. Hwy. 520-2B & 17 (Service Rd). Tel.: (514) 739-3391. S $16.50–; D $21–.

Holiday Inn. 420 Sherbrooke W. (Hwy. 2). Tel.: (514) 842-6111. S $18–; D $24–.

Holiday Inn—Seigneurie. 7300 Cote de Liesse. Exit 19 S. from Trans-Canada Hwy. Tel.: (514) 731-7751.. S $16.50–; D $21–.

Sheraton-Mount Royal Hotel. 1455 Peel St. Tel.: (514) 842-7777. S $13–; D $18–. Small pets.

QUEBEC

Holiday Inn. Hochelaga, Quebec 10. Intersection Hwys. 2 & 9. Tel.: (418) 653-4901. S $13.50–; D $18–.

Motel Carillon Hotel. On Hwys. 1, 2, 3, 5, 9, 20 at 2800 Blvd. Laurier. Tel.: (418) 653-5234. S $12.50–; D $16–.

Saskatchewan

PRINCE ALBERT

Sheraton-Marlboro Motor Inn. First Ave. E. & 13th St. Tel.: (306) 763-2644. S $10.50–; D $14.50–. Small pets.

REGINA

Holiday Inn. 777 Albert. Tel.: (306) 527-0121. S $10.50–; D $13.50–.

SASKATOON

Sheraton-Cavalier Motor Inn. 612 Spadina Crescent. Tel.: (306) 652-6770. S $12– D $16–.

FRANCE

Paris has the hard-won reputation of being a rather unfriendly place for the American tourist. There is certainly ample evidence to support the notion that the Parisian is not the person most likely to go out of his or her way to make you feel at home. (Of course, if you come from New York that in itself will probably make you feel right at home!) Traveling around Paris with a dog, however, proved to me (Paula) an unexpectedly pleasant experience. Perhaps it is quite a simple thing, this acceptance of oneself as a tourist when accompanied by a dog. So many European cities are noticeably almost "taken over" during the summer months by tourists and many of these tourists are from the United States. English is heard almost more often than French is in the more well traveled areas of Paris. If you are with your dog you become again an individual and not just part of what must seem an invading horde. Not only are you yourself more related to your everyday life with your pet at your heels, but strangers can more easily respond to you as an individual human being.

Most restaurants in Paris will permit dogs to enter. There are a few that prohibit them, but in a city of so many marvelous restaurants this poses only a minor problem. Most shops also permit dogs to enter, although food shops, particularly the *charcuteries,* are apt to ask you to leave your dog outside. If you have a dog small enough to pick up and carry, then you can take it into such shops. For you who own small dogs or cats, travel on public transport is possible so long as you put the pet in a basket or carrying case. Obviously for some of us this is out of the question. Louie, for instance, would fit comfortably into a steamer trunk, but I just don't travel around with one under my arm! So the autobus and metro are out for large dogs. Taxis, of course, are generally happy to accept dogs but do take a look to see what is sitting next to the driver. I have found that, particularly in the evening, Parisian taxi drivers are apt to have dogs riding with them on the front seat. Having been assured by one driver not to worry about his little dachshund and to enter the cab, I walked toward the door. As soon as I moved toward it this little red dog jumped out of the window of the cab and

Your pet might enjoy a new taste or beverage.

started to attack my considerably larger but rather mild-mannered beast. We both ran and escaped with no injury but with an eye schooled to check the front seats of cabs.

While dogs are not permitted in movie theaters they are permitted in parks (appropriately enough, you might think). However, you must keep your dog on a leash while you are in the park, and if you don't, you will be asked rather quickly to leave.

Hotels

It is not our purpose to give here a complete list of every hotel that will accept a dog. In fact, we don't have enough space to list every hotel in Paris that will accept dogs, so we certainly cannot mention hotels in other cities or throughout the provinces. What follows is a geographically distributed list of hotels in Paris accepting dogs. During the tourist season (June, July and August), hotels in Paris are heavily booked, so we suggest that you try to make advance reservations. Paris is divided into 20 districts called *arrondissements.* We will list two hotels for most *arrondissements;* where possible they will be in differing price categories.

1^e
Hôtel Montpensier
12 Rue de Richelieu
Tel.: 742-54-34

Mary Hôtel
32 Rue Ste. Anne
Tel.: 742-25-67

2^e
Hôtel François
3 Blvd. Montmartre
Tel.: 231-98-30

Hôtel Île de France*
26 Rue St. Augustin
Tel.: 742-40-61

3^e
Paris-Bruxelles*
4 Rue Meslay
Tel.: 272-71-32

Hôtel Plat d'Étain
69 Rue Meslay
Tel.: 887-04-04

(Nothing for 4ᵉ and 5ᵉ
arrondissements)

6ᵉ

Hôtel Pas-de-Calais*
59 Rue Sts. Pères
Tel.: 548-78-74

Hôtel d'Isly
29 Rue Jacob
Tel.: 326-64-41

7ᵉ

Hôtel Sofitel-Bourbon
32 Rue St. Dominique
Tel.: 555-21-11

Hôtel St. Germain
88 Rue du Bac
Tel.: 548-62-92

8ᵉ

Hôtel George V
31 Avenue George V
Tel.: 225-35-30

Hôtel Printemps*
1 Rue Isly
Tel.: 387-35-44

9ᵉ

Le Grand Hôtel
2 Rue Scribe
Tel.: 742-75-79

Hôtel Montholon-Lafayette*
4 Rue Riboutté
Tel.: 770-36-72

10ᵉ

Hôtel Paix*

2 bis Blvd. St. Martin
Tel.: 607-40-56

Hôtel Pavillon
36 Rue Echiquier
Tel.: 770-17-15

11ᵉ

Place Voltaire
132 Blvd. Voltaire
Tel.: 700-39-83

12ᵉ

Azur
5 Rue Lyon
Tel.: 343-88-35

Stade
111 Blvd. Poniatowski
Tel.: 343-30-38

13ᵉ

Rubens
35 Rue Banquier
Tel.: 402-73-30

Arts
8 Rue Coypel
Tel.: 331-22-30

14ᵉ

Midi
4 Avenue René-Coty
Tel.: 707-70-16

Oriental
1 Avenue Général Leclerc
Tel.: 331-64-65

Hôtel Virginia*
66 Rue Père-Corentin
Tel.: 707-70-36

15^e
Institut Hôtel
23 Blvd. Pasteur
Tel.: 734-41-51

Rosaria Hôtel
42 Blvd. Garibaldi
Tel.: 783-20-10

16^e
La Pérouse
40 Rue la Pérouse
Tel.: 727-43-68

Union Hôtel Étoile
44 Rue Hamelin
Tel.: 553-14-95

17^e
Balmoral
6 Rue Général Lanrezac
Tel.: 380-30-50

Belfast*
10 Avenue Carnot
Tel.: 380-12-10

18^e
De Flore
108 Rue Lamarck
Tel.: 606-31-15

(Nothing for 19e and 20^e
arrondissements)

* *the less-expensive hotel*

GERMANY, FEDERAL REPUBLIC OF

According to the Tierschutzbund, the German equivalent of the A.S.P.C.A., there are three million dogs and an equal number of cats owned as pets in Germany today. So you needn't fear a shortage of supplies or services for your animal. Grooming services, pet shops and prepared pet food are widely available in all cities. In smaller towns and rural areas, you will probably have to do without grooming services. It's also possible you may have to substitute fresh meat from the local butcher for canned pet food. But this is not particularly difficult to do and people, either in your hotel or in the shops, will gladly help you.

Veterinarians abound throughout Germany and you'll find them listed in the classified section of telephone directories. Women's liberationists will be pleased to know that the field of veterinary medicine has opened up for women in recent years and German women have responded enthusiastically to their new opportunity.

Much of what we consider public transport is privately owned in Germany and, therefore, no consistent ruling was available. You will probably be able to travel on buses and streetcars with your pet if you have it in a carrier and can hold it on your lap or place it under your seat. If, in your own travels, you find any areas that are more liberal in their rulings on larger pets, please write to us about them. The German Federal Railroad is very considerate of animals, although they do insist that an animal be accompanied by its health documents. Small pets may either be held on your lap or be in a suitable container as long as the other passengers do not object. There are special compartments in both first and second class where you are permitted to travel with a pet of any size. However, should other passengers complain, the conductor will escort you and your pet to the baggage car, which is equipped with built-in kennels where you may leave your animal to be competently looked after by the baggageman. Dogs cost half of a second-class ticket regardless of what class ticket you're traveling on.

Hotels will often accept small dogs, cats or birds, but it is considerably more difficult for larger pets. We urge that you make your reservations in advance, if possible. If you decide, on the spur of the moment, to travel in Germany or you anticipate difficulty because of your pet's size, contact the nearest tourist office for the Tierschutzbund's list of kennels and pet hotels. Or you can write to them directly: Tierschutzbund, President Wolfgang Kiemer, Albinistrasse 11213, 6500 Minz, Germany.

Most teashops, cafés and restaurants will allow you to bring your pet. If you've been out for a long day's shopping or sight-seeing, you needn't rush back to the hotel to leave your animal. As usual, it's the individual proprietor's decision and you may encounter a few refusals, but there's bound to be another place nearby that will permit you both. If you're planning on an evening out, we suggest you check in advance with the restaurants that interest you to avoid last-minute disappointments and hard feelings.

GREECE

Dogs and cats are *not allowed* to travel on buses, trains or boats unless they are in carrying cases or kennels. Most hotels do accept dogs and cats, as do many restaurants.

ITALY

Italy is everywhere delightful, and for the pet owner it is an especially charming country. I (Geraldine) bought my dog Twiggy when I was living in Rome and can attest that it's a much more easygoing city to raise a pet in than New York proves to be.

For one thing, you are allowed to take your pet with you practically everywhere. Eating out is one of the mainstays of Italian social life and Twiggy was always permitted in cafés, bars, ice-cream parlors and restaurants. The only objection ever raised was from one owner's cat that rushed from its corner, smacked Twiggy in the face and then stalked back to finish its nap. We were too astonished to do anything but leave; however, it's more usual for an owner to place his cat where it's not likely to quarrel with your dog.

You'll find that there's a greater danger that your dog will be overfed rather than undernourished in Italy. People are always eager to ply your pet with food. Restaurant owners and waiters will often ask if they can bring water or food for your dog—sometimes they just bring it. So if you've arrived in town too late to shop for dog food or have just simply forgotten about it, you can always get a square meal for your dog at the nearest restaurant. Restaurants usually serve lunch from noon to 3 P.M. and dinner from 7 or 8 P.M. until midnight. The only thing that might give offense is if you were to give your pet your own plate to eat from. The general feeling is that animals should eat from newspaper or from a plate or bowl not used to serve human beings, although once I ordered Twiggy an ice cream that she ate from a little silvered dish, just as I did, but I don't recommend it as a regular practice.

One further thing on the subject of food: On a recent trip to Italy, I found that canned pet food was more commonly available than it was when I lived there. However, you may find yourself in an area where there is none. In that case, you can substitute their tinned beef, called Simmenthal, which is very nourishing and palatable. You can also buy fresh meat and bones at the butcher's. Each butcher shop specializes in one animal's meat only, i.e., there is a butcher shop for beef, one for horsemeat, one for lamb, etc. I suggest you stick to lamb, beef or horsemeat. The latter, by the way, is considered for human consumption so it is not any cheaper than other meats. Butchers will gladly accommodate you with scraps and cheap cuts if you tell them it's for your pet. But, by way of good international relations, if you do intend a more expensive cut of meat for your pet be tactful and don't mention it. As for biscuits, there are many nonsweetened, fairly hard babies' teething biscuits available that make good substitute treats.

The only places where your pet is firmly forbidden entry are museums, historic ruins and zoos. I say "firmly forbidden" because, like prices, Italian rules and regulations are often quite flexible. If someone is reluctant to allow your dog entry, never immediately accept a No. Extol your pet's virtues, talk about what a wonderful creature it is—so clean, so well-behaved—and how sad you'll be if you're turned away. You have nothing to lose by a little friendly discussion and, usually, everything to gain. As far as one can generalize, Italians don't mind being persuaded to change their minds or make an exception from the generosity of their hearts. However, if your coaxing only arouses greater formality, don't persist.

There is almost a national passion against cutting a *brutta figura,* meaning being embarrassed or looking foolish. When someone continues to refuse, you'll do better to drop the issue and thank him anyway for his kindness. Chances are that he will not only apologize profoundly for disappointing you but may then permit your pet to enter to avoid seeming hardhearted.

You may never have an opportunity to experience this type of bargaining. Practically every hotel, from the smallest *pensione* to the grandest *albergo,* will accept your pet, often with no further ado than that you agree to pay for any damage it might cause.

Your pet may travel on buses, trams and subways if it's in a carrier, or in the case of a dog, if it's muzzled. Train regulations stipulate that your dog must be muzzled if it's in the compartment with you. I always take a muzzle along but, frankly, neither Twiggy nor Lorenzo has had to wear one yet. There *is* one precaution, however, you should definitely take in regard to train travel in Italy. Reserve your seat in advance, especially if you're traveling second class. It will probably mean waiting in line for an hour the day before your trip, but it's well worth it. Standing or jammed in the aisle among parcels and suitcases all the way from Venice to Rome just isn't the quintessence of traveling pleasure. And it happens . . . all the time; no matter what the season there always seems to be more passengers than seats. Except for a TEE train (Trans Europe Express), all trains in Europe permit dogs, and in Italy, your dog's fare will cost half of a second-class ticket.

Where else can you take your pet? Well, Twiggy has been to movies and concerts (and, fortunately, she slept through them) and shopping in small stores, outdoor markets and large department stores. She also traveled by both hydrofoil and ferry from Naples to Capri and Ischia and was welcome to play on the exquisite beaches there. Lake fronts and beaches are generally parceled out among many concessions, each of which has its own beach area, changing cabins, and indoor/outdoor restaurant. Most will accept pets, but if one place objects, it's a simple matter to continue down the road to the next, more accommodating concession. If you're near Venice and/or Ferrara, you might want to visit the Lido delle Nazione, a large resort complex that features a beach exclusively for dogs. They provide deck chairs especially constructed for dogs, as well as umbrellas, beach balls and even bones. An attendant with a bucket and shovel keeps the place tidy. It costs approximately $1.30 per day for your dog to enjoy these pleasures; food is extra and the price depends on how much your dog consumes. The dog's sector is right next to a beach for people, so you may watch over your pet if you want to. Hotel officials report that they've had no trouble so far and are not expecting any because the beach has been carefully designed to prevent dogs from fighting among themselves or from congregating in packs.

You can judge for yourself that Italy is an extremely tolerant country. Whether or not you take your pet on any outing will usually be up to you to decide on the basis of your own mood and your animal's size, temperament and its possible reactions to the situations you're considering. For example, suppose you want to spend Sunday morning shopping at Porto Portese, Rome's flea market. You may decide to leave your dog at home if it's small and a nuisance to carry or if it reacts badly to crowds, whereas it might be perfectly all right to take along a larger or more placid dog. But, with or without your pet, you should pay the flea market a visit. It's a very lively scene, with sword swallowers and fire-eaters and hundreds of stalls selling junk mixed in with excellent bargains and very lovely antiques. In the middle section there's a fairly extensive animal market selling puppies of mixed breeds, fish, rabbits, kittens, and brightly colored Bengalini, which are very small, delightful tropical birds.

And the last, but not least, item of importance is that veterinarians and grooming services are also generally available. If you have trouble coping with the telephone directory, don't hesitate to ask for help from hotel personnel, tourist offices, even people on the street who may just stop what they're doing and take you there themselves. If you're in Rome and want competent service from an English-speaking doctor, consult Dr. Robert Bowler, veterinarian to the stars. Located midway between the center of Rome and Cinecittà and De Laurentiis' studios, Dr. Bowler has tended to everything from Elizabeth Taylor Burton's ailing Pekinese to a stray kitten rescued by producers Ninki Maslanski and Mel Frank. Fortunately, Dr. Bowler's prices are not as stellar as his clientele tends to be, and you can have your pet doctored, groomed or boarded for quite modest sums. If you need him, he's at Viale Porta Ardeatina 57, Rome; telephone: 577-8268.

JAPAN

The Japanese tend to favor birds and crickets as pets and therefore are not particularly geared to a dog and cat population. You'll find pet shops in the larger cities where you will be able to buy supplies and pet food but the food for animals is limited both in quantity and variety. If you're traveling with a cat, it's an easy matter to substitute raw, dried or cooked fish, which you can buy at street stands, stores or restaurants. The same substitution is possible for dogs as well, if your dog likes fish—and most do. Just be careful to check the fish to be sure there are no bones your pet might choke on. Otherwise, you should simply stock up in advance of your trip on the lightweight nonperishable variety of pet food when you are traveling to Japan directly from the United States or any other country where pet food is readily obtainable.

Again, because of the differences in pet preferences, Japanese hotels do not expect dogs or cats with their visitors and it is necessary to contact the hotel of your choice in advance for permission to bring your animal.

There is no lack of fine veterinarians so you may easily contact one for help or advice should the need arise.

Animals are not permitted in restaurants, and only small animals in carriers may be taken on public transport. Japanese railroads allow you to carry your pet with you in coaches if it's in a case measuring no more than 1′ x 1′ x 1′, and the cost is a nominal 25 cents. They do not accept pets weighing more than 10 kilos (22 pounds) and will not carry an animal any distance greater than 100 kilometers (62 miles). Therefore, whether traveling by train is easy for you or not will depend on the size of your pet or the distance you plan to cover.

MEXICO

You'll find everything you need for your pet—i.e., food, pet shops, veterinarians and grooming services—in any Mexican city. The smaller towns and villages may not be so adequately stocked in prepared pet foods and the like and, therefore, you should either lay in a supply before setting out or plan on substituting locally available fresh meat for your pet's regular diet.

The rules regarding public transportation are very much the same as for the United States. You are allowed to take your animal onto a bus, streetcar or subway only if it's in a carrying case. The Mexican Railway System carries pets in baggage cars only and you must have your pet's health certificate attesting that it has been vaccinated with rabies serum.

Most hotels do permit people to bring their pets but with the proviso that the client is to be responsible for any damage caused by his animal. Usually, it's wiser to ask in advance whether or not a hotel will allow you in with your animal but, for emergencies and just general information, here is a list of Mexican hotels that definitely welcome pets.

ACAPULCO

Holiday Inn Off-Shore Resort Inn. Costera Miguel Alemán #1260. Tel.: 4-04-10. S $18–; D $22–.

CULIACÁN

Los Tres Rios. On Mexico Hwy. #15. Carretera Internacional KM 1425; Apartado Postal 242. Tel.: 2-30-31. S $10–; D $14–.

GUADALAJARA

Camino Real. Vallarta 5005. Tel.: 15-73-30. S $16–; D $20–.
Holiday Inn. Corner Lopez Mateos and M. Otero. Tel.: 16-84-00. S $14–; D $16–.

MATAMOROS

Holiday Inn. Cinco and Miguel Alemán Avenida. Tel.: 2-36-00. S $12–; D $14–.

MAZATLÁN

Master Hosts Inn. Located directly on the beach. For additonal information call (213) 877-0783, Master Hosts International.

MEXICO CITY

Holiday Inn. Blvd. Pto. Aereo No. 502. Tels. 5-22-62-64; 5-22-56-11; 5-22-57-93; 5-22-58-41. S $16–; D $19–.

Maria Barbara Motel. On Hwy. 57, north of Satelite City. Tels.: 62-21-03 and 62-02-29. S $6.80–; D $9.20–.

MONTERREY

Holiday Inn. Avenida Universidad 101. Tel.: 52-24-00. S $14–; D $16–.

Ramada Inn. Avenida Topo Chico. P.O. Box 249. Tel.: 53-86-70. S $10–; D $12–.

MOROCCO

Pets are permitted to travel on public transportation and are allowed in many restaurants and hotels. In general there are no special shops catering to the needs of pets, although you will be able to find such items as leashes and collars in large shops in the biggest cities. Food will have to be purchased from butchers and for this you might want to consult the French vocabulary section of this book. The following is a list of hotels that definitely accept dogs. There are other hotels in Morocco that accept pets, but the policy will vary with each hotel. (We do not, of course, endorse these hotels; this is simply a list of those hotels where we know the fixed policy vis-à-vis pets. The following are all Holiday Inns.)

Single = S   Double = D

CASABLANCA

Place Mohammed V
Innkeeper: Frank Hartmann
S $14–; D $16–.

FEZ

Avenues des Far and Allal Ben Abdellah
Tel.: 230-06
S $11–; D $13–.

MARRAKECH

Avenues de France and de la Menera
Tel.: 300-76.
S $11–; D$13–.

TANGIER

Bay of Tangier at Malabata
Innkeeper: Roberto Giansoldati
S $14–; D $16–.

NETHERLANDS

Traveling in the Netherlands with my (Paula's) dog has been a new and lovely experience. Unlike New York, our usual domicile (if New York could ever be considered a usual place), dogs are permitted on buses, trams, trains and boats throughout this small country. One needs no special equipment, i.e., carrying cases or muzzles. What you must do is pay half fare for each dog regardless of its size. Several tram conductors have jokingly asked me to pay a full fare since I have a rather large dog, but a joke it was and it's been half fare for him all the way. We have never been turned away from a restaurant and most stores permit dogs as well. Once in a great while a store owner will insist that the dog be kept outside and this usually is a food store. However, I have discovered that it is usually not the produce that is being protected. Rather it is the owner's cat! Being a New Yorker I had quite forgotten, of course, that in the unusual event of dog prohibition all I had to do was tie the dog outside the shop. I had been so afraid of "dognapers" that I had completely forgotten that this is not a world-wide problem. In fact, on these rare occasions, dogs have garnered as much attention outside shops as they could probably bear.

There are several places in Amsterdam where dogs are prohibited. These are the Rijksmuseum (so Fido will have to miss Rembrandt), the Stedelijk Museum (missing modern art as well) and the zoo. I had been told the cinemas don't permit dogs to enter but this is a question where some common sense and local custom come in. If you have a small dog, like a dachshund or mini-poodle, it will probably be permitted in the movie theater. I have seen an Irish setter in a movie theater, so it seems that it is in part a question of trying and seeing what happens. Naturally, if you have a dog that tends to bark when it is in strange places, it would be better to leave the dog in your room or skip the movies.

Because we have dogs that have led relatively restricted urban lives this freedom of movement was a new opportunity to find out more about their character. Fortunately, we have found our dogs to be adaptable to all kinds of new situations and they have presented few problems. Louie, for example, upon entering a tram, bus or train compartment simply finds a comfortable spot near my (Paula's) seat, curls up and goes to sleep. Louie used to drool from fear when riding in a car, so touring has made him quite a sensible and sophisticated traveler.

The Dutch are well known for being a most tolerant people and this tolerance extends to animals and regulations pertaining to them. For example, there are parks that forbid the entry of dogs unless they are kept on a leash. One observes that these parks are filled with freely running dogs. Entrances to the beach at Zandvoort have signs prohibiting dogs and yet there are many dogs at the beach busy fetching sticks out of the North Sea. It is not suggested that anyone break the law. What we suggest is that you obey local custom and do let common sense and knowledge of your pet determine your actions. It seems that there is simply no objection to these rules being disregarded. So long as you don't have a particularly aggressive dog there's no need to keep it on a leash in the park. If your dog likes to run kicking up sand instead of swimming after sticks, then take it to an uncrowded part of the beach. Not only do you and your dog avoid trouble in this fashion, you also, of course, will be maintaining a pleasant situation for the local people.

Hotels

In keeping with the feeling of hospitality to pets and their owners, you will find that many hotels in Holland accept pets. We had become so used to having an easy time traveling through Holland with our dogs that when making a reservation to spend the weekend at a seaside hotel, it completely slipped our minds to check whether they accepted dogs. Things turned out well enough since not a word was said when we arrived and we all had a marvelous time sailing on the IJsselmeer. Certainly check if you're not sure what a given hotel's pet policy is since obviously you wouldn't want to travel only to be disappointed. We do, however, mean to relay the information that traveling in both Amsterdam and the countryside of the Netherlands is easy and fun with your pets. There is no need to expect the slightest difficulty in getting accommodations. The VVV (Tourist Information Center) in Amsterdam has a book listing all the hotels in the Netherlands and their pet policies are included with the listing. If you plan to travel into the countryside we recommend that you buy this book. It costs the equivalent of about 80 cents.

Pet Shops

Many people in Holland have pets and lavish a great deal of care on them. There are many shops specializing in food and goodies for the dog and the cat. Unlike pet shops in the United States, *Hundwinkels* in Holland, for example, don't sell pets at all. They simply sell the necessities and luxuries for a fine dog's (or cat's) life. Each area of Amsterdam has at least one such shop. You will find all manner of things here—special biscuits, meal for breakfast, food that is especially for dogs that are having digestive troubles, several varieties of canned dog and cat food and fresh meat for dogs and cats. Most of the shops also carry at least one "American" brand of dry dog and cat food. They, of course, also sell dog beds and all types of collars and leashes, as well as vitamin products and grooming aids, so if you forgot to pack your dog's very own brush there is nothing to worry about—you will be able to choose from a wide selection of different type brushes.

While most people in Amsterdam speak at least a little English, sometimes owners of small shops that don't especially cater to tourists do not know English. Please don't let the language barrier keep you from going to a *Hundwinkel* since we have always found that people staffing them to be particularly friendly and helpful. Since these shops are unlike pet shops in America you would also be missing an especially Dutch (or at least foreign) phenomena and that too would be a shame. Many of these shops also offer grooming services such as clipping and bathing. If the particular one you stop at doesn't offer these services and you would, for example, like your dog to have a bath, you can ask their advice about special places for dog grooming as these are also widely available.

Supermarkets and grocery stores usually carry more than one brand of canned dog food and canned cat food. They sometimes also sell different types of dog biscuits. The street markets such as that on Albert Cuypstraat have stalls that sell pet foods as well, and these markets are cheaper for most items than are the shops. However, the street-market stalls generally sell pet food for cats, birds and fish more often than food for dogs. In street markets, supermarkets and *Hundwinkels* you will also easily find special preparations for your cat's litter box.

The following is a list of geographically dispersed *Hundwinkels* in Amsterdam. Check with someone at your hotel, or with your map, to see which is nearest you. Remember that Amsterdam is a small city so that at least one of these shops should be quite near the place where you're staying. The VVV on the Rokin is staffed with helpful and well-informed

Introduce your pet to other pets.

people, so if there are any questions you have concerning your pet as well as the rest of your visit to Holland, don't hesitate to phone them or stop in. We have also found the people who staff the telephone information service to be helpful and interested as well. When looking for a place to board our dogs, we found some problems because the summer months are the times when many pet-owning Dutch families go on holidays and many kennels had been booked solid some months ahead. Since we couldn't go to Britain unless the dogs were boarded, we became a little desperate. The personnel at information were fantastically helpful and gave us a variety of numbers for kennels near Amsterdam. The first we called was perfect and our dogs too enjoyed a lovely holiday.

DIERENBENODIGDHEDEN (Shops selling animal food and supplies)

J. G. de Winter*
7 van Woustraat
Tel.: 79-40-01

Dierenparadijs
Centuurbaan 61
Tel.: 72-34-57

Dog's Toilet Shop
11 Emmastraat
Tel.: 72-34-25

F. A. Geuzebroek
23-25 Marnixstraat
Tel.: 24-77-43

de Meeuw
23 Meeuwenplein
Tel.: 27-88-26

Moe Voskamp
58 Tilanusstraat
(hk Kamperstraat)
Tel.: 94-77-98

G. Koning
Nieuw Leliestraat 88
Tel.: 24-17-64

Dog Service
444 Prinsengracht
Tel.: 13-24-40

J. J. Wentzel
14 K Reguliersdwarstraat
Tel.: 23-08-39

* Mr. de Winter's shop provided Louie with his meals for some months. The people were friendly, helpful and just generally nice to us.

The following is a list of veterinarians in Amsterdam. As with the above list of shops, it is not complete but does give a representative geographical listing.

DIERENARTSEN (Veterinarians)

A. H. M. Erken
135 Weteringschans
Tel.: 22-18-84

E. C. Osinga**
2a hs Uithoornstraat
Tel.: 79-60-35

W. de Haan
518 Overtoom
Tel.: 18-28-84

** Dr. Osinga and his staff speak English. Louie was well cared for when he suffered from tonsillitis (brought on by too much swimming in the North Sea!).

PUERTO RICO

It's lovely and your pet might enjoy the sun and sea as much as you will but there *are* a few problems—transportation, for one. Pets are not permitted on any public transport or in taxis. That means you'll have to walk or rent a car.

Most hotels do not accept pets, but this is not an insurmountable obstacle. It implies that some *do,* and you'll be able to find accommodations—quite nice ones, at that. We know for a fact that the Americana in San Juan accepts miniature dogs at no extra charge.

As to eating out with your animal friend, it's welcome at outdoor cafés and, despite the law to the contrary, many restaurant owners allow pets in.

Boarding, grooming and veterinary services are available on the island. San Juan has a clinic called Emergency Veterinary Services, which is open 24 hours a day. Should you need them, their telephone number is 724-3013, extension 227.

SPAIN

Few people in Spain keep pets as such. Dogs, for instance, would be kept as guard animals and cats as catchers of mice or rats. Because few pets are kept simply as companions, there are few special facilities for them. Unless your pet is kept in a travel carrier, you will not be able to take it on public transportation. In almost any city and certainly in smaller towns, you will have to buy food at either a butcher shop or fish store. While there are no special shops selling leashes and flea powder, you will find a section in larger department stores selling such items. Whether or not a restaurant will accept your dog or cat will depend entirely on the decision of the proprietor. The same holds true for hotels. Many hotels do, however, have a stated policy of accepting pets. Below you will find only a short list of hotels in various price ranges that definitely accept pets. Be aware that many more than these listed do accept pets and this is true for all the cities in Spain.

Single = S   Double = D

BARCELONA

Manila
Ramblas, 111
Tel.: 2320400
S from 250–540 pesos
D from 500–890 pesos

Continental
Ramblas, 140
Tel.: 2228770
S from 140–289 pesos
D from 250–480 pesos

Casa del Médico (Hostel)
Tapineria, 10
Tel.: 2211586
S from 65–100 pesos
D from 110–190 pesos

COLÓN
Avenida Catedral, 9
Tel.: 2228707
S from 260–435 pesos
D from 530–775 pesos

Mesón Castilla
Valdoncella, 5
Tel.: 2313900
S from 130–180 pesos
D from 215–320 pesos

MADRID

Ritz
Paseo del Prado, s/n
Tel.: 2212857
S from 650–815 pesos
D from 975–1,480 pesos

Principe Pio
Onésimo Redondo, 16
Tel.: 2478000
S from 215–219 pesos
D from 320–480 pesos

Amaya (Hostel)
Concepción Arenal, 4
Tel.: 2213618
S from 75–100 pesos
D from 125–190 pesos

Santa Clara (Hostel)
Castillejos, 437 and 439
Tel.: 2364931
S from 60–80 pesos
D from 100–180 pesos

Ecuestre
Zurbano, 79
Tel.: 2539400
S from 215–320 pesos
D from 430–545 pesos

Aragón
Nuñez de Arce, 1
Tel.: 2222900
S from 85–110 pesos
D from 140–245 pesos

Garcia (Pension)
Chinchilla, 4
Tel.: 2223269
S from 70–90 pesos
D from 110–150 pesos

UNION OF SOVIET SOCIALIST REPUBLICS

As you will see on page 155, the arrangements for taking your pet into the Soviet Union are simply and easily made. *However*, pets are not, under any circumstances, permitted to stay in hotels! In this case, if you are planning to travel as a regular tourist, you will not be able to take your pet (unless, of course, you don't plan to sleep). If you are planning to go camping, or if you will be staying with friends or relatives, then you can travel with your pet in the U.S.S.R.

Pets are allowed on public transportation and on the railroads.

VIRGIN ISLANDS

Your pet can relax right along with you on these beautiful islands. All the amenities of a pet's life are readily available: pet food; pet shops for supplies you may have left at home; grooming services for sprucing up after playing on the beach; and veterinarians, in case of emergency.

Although you are not permitted to take your animal into an enclosed restaurant, you are welcome with it at any of the many outdoor cafés, where a great portion of the islands' social life is conducted . . . and where your pet will probably be a social asset.

You can take a small pet on public transportation provided it is in a carrier. Large pets are condemned to a life of luxury as they are not allowed to ride in anything except rental cars and taxis.

Another delightful bonus: You and your pet can enjoy camping in the Virgin Islands National Park on lovely Cinnamon Bay. For information about camping facilities, parking, swimming and food service, write the park at Box 806, Charlotte Amalie, St. Thomas, V.I. 00801.

The following hotels accept pets:

ST. CROIX

Christiansted, St. Croix, Virgin Islands, W.I. 00820 (mailing address)

Caravelle Hotel
Club Comanche
Grapetree Bay

King Christian Hotel
The Lodge
Tamarind Reef

Frederiksted, St. Croix, Virgin Islands, W.I. 00840 (mailing address)

Estate Carlton Beach Hotel

ST. JOHN

St. John, Virgin Islands, W.I. (mailing address)

Estate Beth Cruz
Gallows Point
Spyglass Hill

ST. THOMAS

Charlotte Amalie, St. Thomas, Virgin Islands, W.I. 00801 (mailing address)

Indies House
Mandahl Estate Villas
Scotch Beach Hotel
Town House
Tropic Isle Hotel
Virgin Isle Hilton
Water Isle Hotel

FOREIGN WORDS AND PHRASES

The words and phrases in this section are intended as a supplement to any guidebook you will be using when traveling. As we have already suggested, you should of course always feel free to ask people at your hotel or the staff of local tourist agencies any questions you have about the care and feeding of your pet. Don't forget to use the telephone book as well, and for that matter, the operators working at the information number of the telephone system.

This vocabulary section will be of use to anyone who likes to speak the language of the country visited and to anyone who finds herself forced to speak a local language. Since it is meant to be a supplement, you will not find a guide to pronunciation. We assume that by the time you are thinking about your pet's needs you will have had to attend to some of your own and so will be somewhat familiar with the way a given language is spoken.

As you will see, we have reproduced a few words in Greek, Arabic and Hebrew, since these languages use alphabets unlike our own. We hope that these will help both in using telephone directories and in recognizing places you are looking for by the signs outside.

We have included the words and phrases that we have found the most useful and important. As always we are interested in any suggestions from our readers as to additions they feel would help well-traveled pets and their owners.

While you can often get by using sign language, we hope that you do try to use some of these phrases. People in other countries are almost always delighted to have you at least try to speak their language.

FRENCH

Numbers

One	*Un (Une)*
Two	*Deux*
Three	*Trois*
Four	*Quatre*
Five	*Cinq*
Six	*Six*
Seven	*Sept*
Eight	*Huit*
Nine	*Neuf*
Ten	*Dix*

Accessories

Leash	*Laisse*
Collar	*Collier*
Bowl	*Plat*
Brush	*Brosse*
Comb	*Peigne*
Flea powder	*Poudre anti-puces*
Toy	*Jouet*
Travel carrier	*Caisse de voyage pour chien (chat)*

Phrases

I would like a one-way (round-trip) ticket for one dog.
Je voudrais un billet simple (aller-retour) pour un chien.*

Can my cat travel with me?
Est-ce que mon chat** peut voyager avec moi?

Are _____ allowed on trains? (buses, planes, boats, subways, trams)
*Sont-ils autorisés dans les trains? (les autobus, les avions, sur
les bateaux, le metro)*

Do you have something for my _____ to eat?
Avez-vous de la nourriture pour mon _____?

May I have some water for _____?
Puis-je avoir de l'eau pour _____?

Do you accept _____?
Acceptez-vous _____?

Is there any charge?
Devons-nous payer quelque chose?

My _____ is well behaved.
Mon _____ est bien dressé.

Don't be afraid, _____ doesn't bite. (scratch)
N'ayez pas peur, mon _____ ne mord pas. (ne griffe pas)

Please don't tease.
S'il vous plaît, ne le taquinez pas.

_____ likes to play.
_____ est tres joueur.

I'd like a can of dog (cat) food.
Je desirerais une boîte de nourriture pour chien (chat).

I'd like some dog biscuits.
Je desirerais un boîte des biscuits pour chien.

---

* *Le chien* is a male dog; *la chienne* is a female dog. *Une chienne* is the
feminine form for "a dog" or "one dog," and *ma chienne* is the feminine
for "my dog."

** *Le chat* is a male cat; *la chatte* is a female cat. *Une* (one), *la* (the)
and *ma* (my) are the appropriate feminine articles.

Do you have any cheap fresh meat for my _____?
Avez-vous de la viande pour mon _____, pas chère?

Do you have any bones for my dog?
Avez-vous des os pour mon chien?

Can someone walk my dog for an hour? I will pay _____.
*Quelqu'un pourrait-il promener mon chien pour une heure?
Je le payerai _____.*

What do you charge for board? (clipping, trimming nails, bathing)
Quel est le prix d'un chenil? (pour une légère tonte, pour limer ses ongles, pour lui donner un bain)

Where will you keep _____?
Où gardez-vous _____?

May I see it, please?
Puis-je voir l'endroit, s'il vous plaît?

When shall I pick it up?
Quand dois-je le reprendre?

I will be back in _____.
Je serai de retour dans _____.

Where can I find a vet quickly?
Où puis-je trouver rapidement un vétérinaire?

What are your hours?
Quand puis-je venir vous voir avec mon chien (mon chat)?

My _____ needs a sedative. (tranquilizer)
Mon _____ a besoin d'un sédatif. (calmant)

He (She) is vomiting.
Il (Elle) vomit.

He (she) has diarrhea.
Il (Elle) a la diarrhée.

She is in heat.
Elle est en chaleur.

When will he (she) be able to travel?
Quand sera-t-il (elle) en état de voyager?

GERMAN

Numbers

One	*Eins*
Two	*Zwei*
Three	*Drei*
Four	*Vier*
Five	*Fünf*
Six	*Sechs*
Seven	*Sieben*
Eight	*Acht*
Nine	*Neun*
Ten	*Zehn*

Accessories

Leash	*Leine*
Collar	*Halsband*
Bowl	*Schüssel*
Brush	*Bürste*
Comb	*Kamm*
Flea powder	*Insektenpulver*
Toy	*Spielzeug*
Travel carrier	*Tragestasche*

Phrases

I would like a one-way (round-trip) ticket for one dog.
Ich möchte einen Fahrschein (Ruckfahrschein) für einen Hund.

Can my cat travel with me?
Darf mein Katze mit mir reisen?

Are _____ allowed on trains? (buses, planes, boats, subways, trams)

Sind _____ *auf Zügen (Bussen, Flugzeugen, Schiffen, U-Bahnen, Strafenbahnen) zugelassen?*

Do you have something for my _____ to eat?
Haben Sie etwas zu fressen für mein(e) _____?

May I have some water for _____?
Kann ich etwas Wasser haben für _____?

Do you accept _____?
Lassen Sie _____ *zu?*

Is there any charge?
Kostet das etwas?

My _____ is well behaved.
Mein _____ *ist gut erzogen!*

Don't be afraid, _____ doesn't bite. (scratch)
Haben Sie keine Angst, _____ *beisst nicht. (kratzt nicht)*

Please don't tease.
Bitte nicht reizen!

_____ likes to play.
_____ *spielt gern.*

I'd like a can of _____ food.
Ich hätte gerne eine Dose _____ *Nahrung (Schappi).*

I'd like some dog biscuits.
Ich hätte gerne eine Packung Hundekuchen.

Do you have any cheap fresh meat for my _____?
Haben Sie billiges frisches Fleisch für mein(e) _____?

Do you have any bones for my dog?
Haben Sie ein paar Knochen für meinen Hund?

Can someone walk my dog for an hour? I will pay for it.
Kann jemand eine Stunde lang meinen Hund ausführen? Ich werde dafür zahlen.

What do you charge for board? (clipping, trimming nails, bathing)
Was nehmen Sie für Unterbringung und Verpflegung? (Scheren, Nägel kürzen, baden)

Where will you keep _____?
Wo werden Sie _____ unterbringen?

May I see it, please?
Darf ich es bitte sehen?

When shall I pick it up?
Wann kann ich ihn abholen?

I will be back in _____.
Ich werde in _____ zurück sein.

Where can I find a vet quickly?
Wo kann ich schnell einen Tierarzt finden?

What are your hours?
Was sind Ihre Sprechzeiten?

My _____ needs a sedative. (tranquilizer)
Mein _____ braucht ein Beruhigungsmittel.

He (She) is vomiting.
Er (Sie) übergibt sich.

He (She) has diarrhea.
Er (Sie) hat Durchfall.

She is in heat.
Sie ist läufig.

When will _____ be able to travel?
Wann wird _____ wieder reisen können?

ITALIAN

Numbers

One	*Uno*
Two	*Due*
Three	*Tre*
Four	*Quattro*
Five	*Cinque*
Six	*Sei*

Seven	*Sette*
Eight	*Otto*
Nine	*Nove*
Ten	*Dieci*

Accessories

Leash	*Guinzaglio*
Collar	*Collare*
Bowl	*Piatto*
Brush	*Spazzola*
Comb	*Pettine*
Flea powder	*Polvere per le pulci*
Toy	*Giocattolo*
Travel carrier	*Cestino* (basket)

Phrases

I would like a one-way (round-trip) ticket for one dog.
Vorrei un biglietto (di andata e ritorno) per un cane.*

Can my cat travel with me?
Può viaggiare con me il mio gatto?**

Are _____ allowed on trains? (buses, planes, boats, subways, trams)
Si possono portare _____ sul treno? (sull' autobus, sull' aeroplano, sulla nave, sulla metropolitana, sul tram)

Do you have something for my _____ to eat?
Avete qualcosa da mangiare per _____?

May I have some water for _____?
Posso avere dall'acqua per mio _____?

---

* *Un cane* is "a male dog" or "one male dog"; *una cagna* is "a female dog" or "one female dog."
** *Il gatto* is "a male cat"; *la gatta* is "a female cat." *Il mio* is "mine" (masc.); *la mia* is used when the noun is feminine.

Do you accept _____?
Accettate _____?

Is there any charge?
Si paghe qualcosa?

My _____ is well behaved.
Il mio _____ si comporta bene.

Don't be afraid, _____ doesn't bite. (scratch)
Non abbia paura, _____ non morde. (graffia)

Please don't tease.
Per favore, non lo stuzzichi.

_____ likes to play.
Al mio _____ piace giocare.

I'd like a can of _____ food.
Vorrei una scatola di cibo per _____?

I'd like some dog biscuits.
Vorrei una scatola di biscotti per cane.

Do you have any cheap fresh meat for my _____?
Ha della carne fresca a buon prezzo per il mio _____?

Do you have any bones for my dog?
Ha degli ossi per il mio cane?

Can someone walk my dog for an hour? I will pay _____.
*C'è qualcuno che possa portare a spasso il mio cane per un'
ora? Sono disposto(a) a pagare _____.*

What do you charge for board? (clipping, trimming nails,
bathing)
*Quanto costa la pensione? (atosatura, il taglio delle unghie, il
bagno)*

Where will you keep _____?
Dove terrete il mio _____?

May I see it, please?
Posso vederlo, per favore?

When shall I pick it up?
Quando lo dovrei riprendere?

I will be back in _____.
Tornerò tra _____.

Where can I find a vet quickly?
Dove posso trovare un veterinario presto?

What are your hours?
Qual' è il vostro orario?

My _____ needs a sedative. (tranquilizer)
Il mio _____ ha bisogno di un sedativo. (tranquillante)

He (She) is vomiting.
Sta vomitando.

He (She) has diarrhea.
Ha la diarrea.

She is in heat.
È in calore.

When will _____ be able to travel?
Quando sarà _____ in grado di viaggiare?

SPANISH

Numbers

One	*Uno*
Two	*Dos*
Three	*Tres*
Four	*Cuatro*
Five	*Cinco*
Six	*Seis*
Seven	*Siete*
Eight	*Ocho*
Nine	*Nueve*
Ten	*Diez*

No Tenga Miedo Perro No Muerde.

Accessories

Leash	*Correa*
Collar	*Collar*
Bowl	*Plato*
Brush	*Cepillo*
Comb	*Peine*
Flea powder	*Polvo para las pulgas*
Toy	*Juguetes*
Travel carrier	*Bolsa para viaje*

Phrases

I would like a one-way (round-trip) ticket for one dog.
Quiero un billete de ida (de ida y vuelta) para un perro.*

Can my cat travel with me?
¿ Puede viajar mi gato** *conmigo?*

Are _____ allowed on trains? (buses, planes, boats, subways, trams)
¿ Se permiten los _____ en trenes? (autobuses, aviones, barcos, metros, tranvías)

Do you have something for my _____ to eat?
¿ Tiene Vd. algo para que mi _____ pueda comer?

May I have some water for _____?
¿ Podría darme agua para _____?

Do you accept _____?
¿ Usted accepta _____?

Is there any charge?
¿ Cuesta algo?

My _____ is well behaved.
Mi _____ se comporta bien.

* *Perro* is a male dog; *perra* is a female dog.
** *Gato* is a male cat; *gata* is a female cat.

Don't be afraid, _____ doesn't bite. (scratch)
No tenga miedo _____ no muerde. (araña)

Please don't tease.
Por favor, no le moleste.

_____ likes to play.
_____ *le gusta jugar.*

I'd like a can of dog (cat) food.
Quiero una lata de comida para el perro (el gato).

I'd like a box of biscuits.
Quiero una caja de galletas para mi perro.

Do you have any cheap fresh meat for my dog?
¿ Tiene alguna carne barata, fresca para mi perro?

Do you have any bones for my dog?
¿ Tiene alguna huesos para mi perro?

Can someone walk my dog for an hour? I will pay _____.
*¿ Alguién puede pasear me perro por una hora? Pagaré ___
_____.*

What do you charge for board? (clipping, trimming nails,
   bathing)
*¿ Cuánto cobra Vd. por el cuidado? (corte de pelo, corte de
   uñas, baño)*

Where will you keep _____?
¿ Dónde dejará _____?

May I see it, please?
¿ Lo puedo ver, por favor?

When should I pick it up?
¿ Cuándo podría recoger?

I will be back in _____.
Volveré en _____.

Where can I find a vet quickly?
¿ Dónde puedo encontrar un veterinario rápidamente?

What are your hours?
¿ Cuáles son sus horas?

My _____ needs a sedative. (tranquilizer)
Mi _____ necesita un sedativo. (tranquilizante)

He (She) is vomiting.
El (Ella) está vomitando.

He (She) has diarrhea.
El (Ella) tiene diarrea.

She is in heat.
Ella está en celo.

When will _____ be able to travel?
¿ Cuándo podrá viajar _____ ?

PORTUGUESE

Numbers

One	*Um*
Two	*Dois*
Three	*Tres*
Four	*Quatro*
Five	*Cinco*
Six	*Seis*
Seven	*Sete*
Eight	*Oito*
Nine	*Nove*
Ten	*Dez*

Accessories

Leash	*Correia*
Collar	*Coleira*
Bowl	*Tijela*
Brush	*Escova*
Comb	*Pente*
Flea powder	*Pó contra as pulgas*
Toy	*Brinquedo*
Travel carrier	*Cesto de vaigem*

Phrases

I would like a one-way (round-trip) ticket for one dog.
Desejo comprar un bilhete de ida (de ida e volta) para um cão.*

Can my cat travel with me?
O meu gato** pode viajar comigo?

Are _____ allowed on trains? (buses, planes, boats, subways, trams)
São autorizados a viajar nos combóios? (ônibus, aviões, barcos, metropolitanos, carros electricoa)

Do you have something for my _____ to eat?
Têm alguma coisa para ele comer?

May I have some water for _____?
Pode dar-me água para ele beber?

Do you accept _____?
Pode ser aceite?

Is there any charge?
Tenho que pagar alguma coisa?

My _____ is well behaved.
O meu cão e muito obediente.

Don't be afraid, _____ doesn't bite. (scratch)
Não tenha receio, o meo _____ não morde. (arranha)

Please don't tease.
Por favor não o arrelie!

_____ likes to play.
_____ gosta de brincar.

I'd like a can of _____ food.
Gostava de arranjar uma lata de comida para o _____.

I'd like some dog biscuits.
Gostava de arranjar uma lata de biscoitos para o cão.

* *Cão* means a male dog; the word for female dog is *cadela*.
** *Gato* is a male cat; *gata* is a female cat.

Do you have any cheap fresh meat for my _____?
Têm alguma coisa barata? Carne fresca para o _____?

Do you have any bones for my dog?
Têm alguma coisa barata? Ossos para o cão?

Can someone walk my dog for an hour? I will pay _____.
É possivel arranjar alguem de confianca para passear o meu cão durante 1 hora? Estou pronta a pager _____.

What do you charge for board? (clipping, trimming nails, bathing)
Quanto leva por hospedá-lo? (tosquiá-lo, arranjar-lhe as unhas, e dar-lhe banho)

Where will you keep _____?
Onde vai pô-lo?

May I see it, please?
Posso ver, por favor?

When shall I pick it up?
Quando posso ir buscá-lo?

I will be back in _____.
Volto dentro de _____.

Where can I find a vet quickly?
Onde posso arranja urgentemente um veterinário?

What are your hours?
Que horas tem?

My _____ needs a sedative. (tranquilizer)
O meu cão (gato) precisa um calmante.

He (She) is vomiting.
Está a vomitar.

He (She) has diarrhea.
Tem diarreia.

She is in heat.
Ela esta com o cio.

When will _____ be able to travel?
Quando é que pode viajar?

"SIGN LANGUAGE"

Greek

Dog	ΣΚΥΛΟΣ
Cat	ΓΑΤΑ
Veterinarian	ΚΤΗΝΙΑΤΡΟΣ
Pet shop	ΚΑΤΑΣΤΗΜΑ ΓΙΑ
	ΟΙΚΙΑΚΑ ΖΩΑ
	ΔΕΝ ΕΠΙΤΡΕΠΟΝΤΑΙ ΤΑ
No dogs allowed	ΣΚΥΛΙΑ

Arabic (read from right to left)

Dog	كلـب
Cat	قطـة
Veterinarian	دكتور بيطرى
Pet shop	محل لبيع الحيوانات
No dogs allowed	لا يسمح بدخول الكلاب

Hebrew (read from right to left)

Dog	כלב
Cat	חתול
Veterinarian	רופאושרינר
No dogs allowed	לפלבים הכניסה אסורה

BUYING A PET ABROAD

You always wanted an Afghan hound. While traveling through Italy you saw an unusual, beautiful white Afghan puppy. You were going to buy it and then someone told you that there was a quarantine on pets coming into the United States. You missed your opportunity because you were misinformed. You will see in the chapter "Welcome Home!" just what the requirements are for bringing pets into the United States. Because the requirements are easily met, you may consider purchasing a pet on your next foreign trip.

If you select a cat or a dog that is not pedigreed you will need no further information from this chapter. "Welcome Home!" and "International Travel by Plane and Ship" will provide you with all you need to know. If you are planning to buy a more exotic pet, please turn to the end of this chapter and look at the list of endangered species. We are including this list for two reasons. Not only will you have trouble bringing a pet into the United States if it is on the endangered-species list, but you will, by buying such a pet, be participating in the depletion of species already in danger of extinction.

Should you fancy a psittacine bird, please check page 269 for the regulations about bringing it to the United States.

Let's suppose that you want to buy a dog and that it is pedigreed and that for purposes of breeding or showing you want to make sure that you can have it registered with the American Kennel Club when you return to the States. The A.K.C. will consider for registration only those dogs bought in the countries listed below that are registered with the organizations listed. In all cases you must make sure that the certificate of ownership is transferred from the dog's breeder to you before you leave the country of purchase with the dog. Make sure, too, that the pet has been registered by the breeder with the appropriate organization below. When you are ready to register your dog with the A.K.C. you can apply to the dog's breeder for the registration certificate that gives the dog's lineage. The A.K.C. in the United States will send you the application papers for registration.

FOREIGN KENNEL CLUBS

Australia

Australian National Kennel Council
Royal Show Grounds
Ascot Vale
Victoria, Australia

Before any dog can be taken out of Australia, it must receive a veterinary clearance from the Australian Department of Agriculture. Information concerning this clearance can be obtained from the

Department of Agriculture
Quarantine Section
State Office Block
Phillip Street
Sydney, Australia

Austria

Osterreichischer Kynologenverband
Karl Schweighofer-Gasse, 3
A-1070 Vienna, Austria

BELGIUM

>Société Royale Saint-Hubert
>25 Avenue de l'Armée
>Brussels 4, Belgium

CANADA

>The Canadian Kennel Club
>111 Eglinton Avenue East
>Toronto 12, Ontario, Canada
> Registration Division
> P.O. Box 538
> Postal Station F
> Toronto 5, Ontario, Canada

DENMARK

>Dansk Kennelklub
>Norrebrogade, 40
>2200 Copenhagen N., Denmark

If you become a member of this organization you will be entitled to the *Breeder's Guide.*

FINLAND

>Suomen-Kennelliitto-Finska Kennelklubben
>Bulevardi, 14
>Helsinki 12, Finland

This organization will provide you with a list of boarding kennels if you have to board your newly acquired pet for any reason. While they don't have a formal list of breeders, they will be happy to make recommendations if you're looking for a specific breed.

FRANCE

>Société Centrale Canine
>3 Rue de Choiseul
>Paris 2, France

Throughout France there are many kennel clubs dealing with specific breeds. The central society will put you in touch with any specific club and through that club you may obtain a list of breeders.

GERMANY, FEDERAL REPUBLIC OF

There is no central kennel club in Germany. The following is a list of the recognized clubs for each breed.

Affenpinschers; Miniature Pinschers; Miniature, Standard and Giant Schnauzers Only:

Pinscher-Schnauzer-Klub, 1895 e.V.
Gerichtsstrasse 9
62 Wiesbaden, West Germany

Afghan Hounds, Borzois, Greyhounds, Salukis, Whippets Only:

Deutscher Windhundzucht-und Rennverband, e.V.
Werdener Strasse 24
4307 Kettwig/Ruhr, West Germany

Bernese Mountain Dogs of the "Berner Sennenhunde" variety Only:

Schweizer Sennenhundverein für Deutschland (SSV), e.V.
Frau Annemarie Heinzman
8091 Griesstatt
Hochholz, West Germany

Boxers Only:

Boxer Klub, e.V.
Veldenerstrasse 66 (0811)
8-Munich-Pasing, West Germany

Bulldogs Only:

Deutscher Klub für Englische Bulldogs
O-Ing. W. Seemann
7571 Haueneberstein

Am Illgenberg
Baden-Baden, West Germany

Chow-Chows Only:

Allgemeiner Chow-Chow Klub, e.V.
Helmut Haussner
Grafinthaler Strasse 27
6601 Eschringen Saar, West Germany

Collies, Shetland Sheepdogs, Old English Sheepdogs, Pembroke and Cardigan Welsh Corgis Only:

Klub für Britische Hutehunde
Hocken-Heimerstrasse 76
6831 Reilingen, West Germany

Dachshunds Only:

Deutscher Teckelklub, 1888 e.V.
Prinzenstrasse 38
4100 Duisburg, West Germany

Dalmatians Only:

Deutscher Dalmatiner Klub, 1920 e.V.
6980 Wertheim/M-Hofgarten
Unterm Neuberg 13, West Germany

Doberman Pinschers Only:

Doberman-Verein, e.V.
Bahnhofstrasse 116
4705 Pelkum-Wiescherhofen, West Germany

Fox Terriers Only:

Deutscher Fox Terrier-Verband, e.V.
Koloniestrasse 156
41 Duisburg, West Germany

French Bulldogs Only:

Int. Klub für Französische Bulldoggen, e.V.
Romerstrasse 7
8 Munich 28, West Germany

German Shepherd Dogs Only:

> Verein für Deutsche Schäferhunde (SV)
> Beim Schnarrbrunnen, 4
> Augsburg 17, West Germany

German Shorthaired Pointers Only:

> Deutsch Kurzhaar Verband
> den Johannisstrasse 3
> 8500 Nürnberg, West Germany

German Wirehaired Pointers Only:

> Verien Deutsch-Drahthaar, e.V.
> Mr. Georg Greller
> Siegelsdorfer Strasse 18
> 8501 Veitsbronn
> Lkrs. Furth/Bay., West Germany

Great Danes Only:

> Deutscher Doggen Klub, 1888 e.V.
> Winfried Nouc
> Templergraben 16
> 51 Aachen, West Germany

Keeshonden, Pomeranians Only:

> Verein für Deutsche Spitze, e.V. 1899
> Zillestrasse 32
> 4353 Oer-Erkenschwick in Westf., West Germany

Komondorok, Pulik, Kuvaszok Only:

> Klub für Ungarische Hirtenhunde, e.V.
> Salzburger Strasse 10
> 1 Berlin 62 (Schoeneberg), West Germany

Maltese, Pugs, Papillons, Schipperkes, Shih Tzus Only:

> Verband Deutscher Kleinhundezuchter, e.V.
> 8651 Guttenberg 61, Ueber Kulmbach
> Bavaria, West Germany

Newfoundlands Only:

Deutscher Neufundländer-Klub, e.V.
Wittelsbacherstrasse 7
8000 Munich 5, West Germany

Pekingese, Japanese Spaniels Only:

Internationaler Klub für Japan-Chin, Peking-Palast
Hunde und Toy Spaniel, e.V.
Am Lenneberg 20
6507 Ingelheim/Rh., West Germany

Pointers and English, Irish and Gordon Setters Only:

Verein für Pointer und Setter, e.V.
Zuchtbuchamt
Echterstrasse 8
8 Munich 71, West Germany

Poodles Only:

Deutscher Pudel Klub, e.V. (DPK)
Abt. Zuchtbuchamt
Parkstrasse 3
2371 Schulp/Rendsburg, West Germany

Rottweilers Only:

Allgemeiner Deutscher Rottweiler-Klub
Traubenstrasse 58
7000 Stuttgart W., West Germany

St. Bernards Only:

St. Bernard Klub
Frau Irene Michel
8101 Kranzbach/Klais
Oberbayern, West Germany

English Cocker Spaniels, English Springer Spaniels Only:

Jagdspaniel-Klub, e.V.
Zuchtbuchamt
6 Dittmannstrasse
8013 Gronsdorf, West Germany

Airedale Terriers, Bedlington Terriers, Cairn Terriers, Dandie Dinmont Terriers, Irish Terriers, Kerry Blue Terriers, Lakeland Terriers, Manchester Terriers, Scottish Terriers, Sealyham Terriers, Skye Terriers, Welsh Terriers, West Highland White Terriers, Yorkshire Terriers Only:

Klub für Terrier, e.V.
6092 Kelsterbach am Main
Postfach 46, Sitz Frankfurt, West Germany

Weimaraners Only:

Weimaraner Klub, e.V.
4991 Fiestel
Krs. Kubbecke, West Germany

Wirehaired Pointing Griffons Only:

Griffon Klub, e.V. 1888
Forsbacher Strasse 27
5 Köln-Rath, Rhld., West Germany

HUNGARY

Komondorok, Kuvaszok, Pulik and Viszlas Only:

Magyar Ebtenyesztok Orszagos Egyesulete (MEOE)
Wallenberg U.2
Budapest XIII, Hungary

Before you can export a dog bought in Hungary, you will need a permit issued by MEOE as well as a veterinary certificate. If the value of your dog is more than 1,000 Ft. (about $35) you will have to get the permit from:

MAVAD
Hungarian Wild Transporting Company
Budapest I, Hungary

IRELAND

Irish Kennel Club
4 Harcourt Street
Dublin 2, Ireland

Your dog must be more than 8 weeks old before you can get the necessary export papers. The Irish Kennel Club issues these papers for about $7.

ITALY

Ente Nazionale Della Cinofilia Italiana
Viale Premuda 21
20129 Milan, Italy

NETHERLANDS

Raad Van Beheer op Kynologisch
Gebied In Nederland
Emmalaan 16
Amsterdam Z., Netherlands

NEW ZEALAND

The New Zealand Kennel Club
81 Webb Street
Wellington 1, New Zealand

Before you can take your dog out of New Zealand you will need both the certificate of transfer of ownership and a certified export pedigree from the above organization.

NORWAY

Norsk Kennel Klub
Bjorn Farmanns Gate 16
Oslo 2, Norway

The Norsk Kennel Klub suggests that you contact them *before* purchasing a dog. They will help you with information and advice about the kind of dog you want and there is no charge for this service.

SWEDEN

Svenska Kennelklubben
Kungsgatan 51
Stockholm, Sweden

Svenska Kennelklubben is notified by breeders whenever there is a new litter. They will be happy to provide you with this information and anything else that will help you with the purchase and export of your pet. You must get an export certificate from them at a cost of 25 kronor.

SWITZERLAND

> Stammbuchsekretariat der SKG
> Wildparkstrasse 253
> 4656 Wil b. Olten, SO, Switzerland

UNITED KINGDOM

> The Kennel Club
> 1 Clarges Street
> Piccadilly
> London W1, England

If you wish to obtain a list of the registered breeders in the United Kingdom, this organization will send you the *Kennel Gazette,* which costs about 50 cents. They will also send you an application for an export pedigree, which costs about $1.

ENDANGERED SPECIES
Common Name

Mammals

Southern planigale
Little planigale
Dibbler
Large dessert marsupial
   mouse
Long-tailed marsupial mouse
Eastern jerboa—marsupial
Tasmanian tiger
Rusty numbat
Barred bandicoot
Rabbit bandicoot

Lesser rabbit bandicoot
Pig-footed bandicoot
Mountain pigmy possum
Scaly-tailed possum
Barnard's wombat
Brush-tailed rat kangaroo
Lesueur's rat kangaroo
Queensland rat kangaroo
Plain rat kangaroo
Banded hare wallaby
Western hare wallaby

Bridled nail-tail wallaby
Crescent nail-tail wallaby
Parma wallaby
Cuban solenodon
Haitian solenodon
Lemurs—all species
Indris, sifakas, avahis—all
   species
Aye-aye
Spider monkey
Red-backed squirrel monkey
Woolly spider monkey
White-nosed saki
Uakari—all species
Goeldi's marmoset
Golden-rumped tamarin,
   golden-headed tamarin,
   golden lion marmoset
Lion-tailed macaque
Tana River mangabey
Douc langur
Pagi Island langur
Red colobus
Zanzibar red colobus
Kless' gibbon
Pileated gibbon
Orangutan
Gorilla
Brazilian three-toed sloth
Pink fairy armadillo
Brazilian tapir
Volcano rabbit
Mexican prairie dog
False water rat
New Holland mouse

Shark Bay mouse
Shortridge's mouse
Smoky mouse
Western mouse
Field's mouse
Thin-spined porcupine
Northern kit fox
Asiatic wild dog
Mexican grizzly bear
Formosan yellow-throated
   marten
Black-footed ferret
Cameroun clawless otter
La Plata otter
Maned wolf
Giant otter
Barbary hyena
Brown hyena
Asiatic cheetah
Spanish lynx
Barbary serval
Formosan clouded leopard
Asiatic lion
Sinal leopard
Barbary leopard
Anatolian leopard
Bell tiger
Javan tiger
Caspian tiger
Sumatran tiger
Mediterranean monk seal
Dugong
West Indian (Florida)
   manatee
Amazonian manatee

Asian wild ass
African wild ass
Mountain tapir
Central American tapir
Pygmy hog
Vicuña
Swamp deer
Kashmir stag, hangul
Barbary stag
McNeill's deer
Shou
Brow-antlered deer, Eld's
    deer
Persian fallow deer
Bawean deer
Marsh deer
Sonoran pronghorn
Black-faced impala
Clarke's gazelle, dibatag

Swayne's hartebeest
Anoa
Tamaraw
Wood bison
Seladang (gaur)
Wild yak
Kouprey
Banteng
Pyrenean ibex
Walia ibex
Rio de Oro dama gazelle
Mhorr gazelle
Moroccan dorcas gazelle
Cuvler's gazelle
Slender-horned gazelle, Rhim,
    Loder's gazelle
Black lechwe
Arabian oryx

Birds

Galápagos penguin
Arabian ostrich
West African ostrich
Darwin's rhea
Atitlan grebe
Short-tailed albatross
Cahow
Brown pelican
Chinese egret
Oriental white stork
Japanese crested ibis
Aleutian Canada goose
White-winged wood duck
American peregrine falcon

Christmas Island goshawk
Anjouan Island sparrow hawk
Galápagos hawk
Monkey-eating eagle
Spanish imperial eagle
Grenada hook-billed kite
Andean condor
Seychelles kestrel
Mauritius kestrel
Horned guan
Trinidad white-headed
    curassow
Red-billed curassow
LaPerouse's megapode

Maleo
Masked bobwhite
White-eared pheasant
Brown-eared pheasant
Chinese monal
Sclater's monal
Edward's pheasant
Imperial pheasant
Swinhoe's pheasant
Palawan peacock pheasant
Mikado pheasant
Bar-tailed pheasant
Blyth's tragopan
Cabot's tragopan
Western tragopan
Whooping crane
Japanese crane
Siberian white crane
Hooded crane
Auckland Island rail
Kagu
Great Indian bustard
New Zealand shore plover
Eskimo curlew
Audouin's gull
California least tern
Cloven-feathered dove
Chatham Island pigeon
Azores wood pigeon
Grenada dove
Palau ground dove
Ocher-marked parakeet
Kakapo
Red-browed parrot
Bahamas parrot

St. Vincent parrot
St. Lucia parrot
Imperial parrot
Night parrot
Turquoise parakeet
Orange-bellied parrot
Scarlet-chested parrot
Beautiful parakeet
Paradise parakeet
Forbes' parakeet
Mauritius ring-necked
   parakeet
Thick-billed parrot
Red-faced malkoha
Seychelles owl
Palau owl
Mrs. Morden's owlet
Anjouan scops owl
Long-tailed ground roller
Imperial woodpecker
Ivory-billed woodpecker
Tristam's woodpecker
Euler's flycatcher
New Zealand bush wren
Noisy scrubbird
Ponape Mountain starling
Rothschild's starling
Kokako
Piopio
Reunon cuckoo shrike
Mauritius cuckoo shrike
Guadeloupe house wren
St. Lucia wren
Martinique brown trembler
White-breasted thrasher

Mauritius olivaceous bulbul
Cebu black shama
Seychelles magpie robin
Western whipbird
Western bristle-bird
Eyrean grass-wren
Palau fantail
White-necked rock-fowl
Grey-necked rock-fowl
Reed warbler
Rodriguez warbler
Seychelles warbler
Scarlet-breasted robin

Chatham Island robin
Tahiti flycatcher
Tinian monarch
Helmeted honey eater
Seychelles black flycatcher
Seychelles white-eye
Ponape great white-eye
Semper's warbler
Bachman's warbler
Barbados yellow warbler
Kirtland's yellow warbler
São Miguel bullfinch
Slender-billed grachla

Amphibians and Reptiles

Israel painted frog
Stephen Island frog
River terrapin tuntong
Galápagos tortoise
Madagascar radiated tortoise
Hawksbill turtle
Leatherback turtle
Atlantic ridley turtle
South American river turtle
Short-necked or swamp
   tortoise
Yacare

Orinoco crocodile
Cuban crocodile
Morelet's crocodile
Nile crocodile
Gavial
Round Island day gecko
Day gecko
Barrington land lizard
Tuatara
Jamaica boa
Anegada ground iguana

Fish

Ala balik
Cicek
Miyako tanago
Ayumodoki

Mexican blindcat
Nekogigi
Giant catfish
Catfish

Mollusk

Mollusk

WELCOME HOME!

We've met all too many people who confess wistfully that they've always wanted to travel with their pets but never dared face the quarantine hassle upon their return. Or they sadly recount how they passed up the dog of their dreams for a mere pittance overseas compared to what they'd pay for it at home. What, they ask, is our secret? Well, our secret is very simple and we're burning to share it: *There is no quarantine hassle!* In truth, the ease with which your dog or cat gets through U.S. Customs may well give you cause for envy.

U.S. ENTRY REQUIREMENTS

You'll see, as you read this chapter, that the U.S. entry requirements are quite sane and uncomplicated. Most of you have probably already satisfied them in the process of getting your pet ready to leave the country. And the rules are not one whit more difficult for you who have purchased a dog or a cat abroad.

In certain situations, an animal may have to be *confined.* This is definitely not the same as being quarantined. Confinement means that *you,* or an agent selected by you, keep your animal isolated from other animals and from people, except for the contact necessary for its care. The place of confinement can be in your home, in a kennel in your back yard or, if you prefer, under a licensed veterinarian's care. If you allow your animal out of confinement, it must be muzzled and leashed.

And now, read the regulations and cast aside your fears and hesitation.

DOGS

At your port of entry, a quarantine officer will inspect your dog for any evidence of communicable disease.

You will be asked to present your dog's rabies vaccination certificate, signed by a licensed veterinarian. This document should state your dog's name, color, breed, any other identifying remarks, the date it was vaccinated and the type of vaccine used.

Rabies vaccinations are valid as follows:

Nerve-tissue vaccine: at least 1 month and not more than 12 months before arrival.

Chick-embryo vaccine: at least 1 month but not more than 3 years before arrival.

Puppies 3 months old or less are admitted but you will have to certify that you'll keep your pup in confinement until it's vaccinated and for 30 days thereafter. The United States absolutely does not recognize rabies vaccination administered to a dog less than 3 months old. So if you bought the puppy overseas—and presumably you did—don't bother to vaccinate it.

There are no rabies vaccination requirements for:

(a) puppies less than 3 months old, as explained above.
(b) a wild member of the dog family. If you've bought a wild dog, it will be admitted and you must certify that you will keep it in confinement for at least 6 months.

*Don't hide your pet. Immigration authorities
inspect all parcels carefully.*

(c) a dog that has spent the past 6 months in a country listed by the Public Health Service as rabies-free:

Australia	New Zealand
Bahama Islands	Northern Ireland
Bermuda Islands	Norway
Fiji	Sweden
Iceland	Taiwan (Formosa)
Ireland	United Kingdom of
Jamaica	Great Britain
Japan	

Import duty, as of January 1, 1972, on a dog purchased abroad is 3½% of its purchase price. You may include this in your duty-free allowance.

What if You've Lost Your Dog's Rabies Vaccination Certificate?

It's annoying and it will cost you money you'd rather not spend, but it's not the end of the world. You must arrange for and pay the expense of a rabies vaccination immediately upon arrival. As soon as your dog has been vaccinated, it will be admitted but you will have to keep it in confinement for at least 30 days.

What if Your Dog Was Vaccinated Less Than 30 Days Before Arrival?

It's conceivable that if you took your dog with you on a 21-day excursion, you might wind up back in the United States with a valid certificate that was executed less than a month prior to entry. In that case, your dog will be admitted if you swear you'll keep it in confinement until at least 30 days have elapsed since its vaccination.

CATS

To the U.S. government, *cats* means all domestic and wild members of the cat family. And, whether you're coming home with a Persian or a puma, you need only present your cat to the quarantine officer's appraising eye. If your pet shows no evidence of communicable disease, it's home free—unless you bought it overseas. Then there's an *import duty* of 3½% of its purchase price. This can be included in your duty-free allowance, however.

BIRDS

Things are a bit more complicated for the owner of a *psittacine* bird. *Before* you leave the United States, you must obtain a permit from the Surgeon General, Public Health Service, Department of Health, Education, and Welfare, Washington, D.C. 20201. In your application, state the number and description of your birds and list your itinerary.

When you return, your bird will be inspected to see if it's free from communicable diseases. You will then have to present your permit to the quarantine officer *and* certify that your bird will be treated for 45 days with chlortetracycline, or other medication approved by the Surgeon General, under the supervision of a licensed veterinarian. A word to the wise: Be sure to have a letter from your vet saying that he intends to supervise this treatment when you return.

Importing Psittacine Birds

The United States allows members of a single household to import as many as 2 psittacine birds each year. The birds must be free from any signs of communicable disease, and they must be intended as pets and not for sale or trade.

The *import duty* on psittacine birds is 4½% (it dropped

from 17%) as of January 1, 1972. This, too, can be covered by your duty-free allowance.

Well, suppose you've been dying to have a pet parrot and suspect the chances are pretty good that you'll buy one while you're abroad. Get a written statement from your vet *before* you leave that says that he's willing to supervise or administer treatment to your pet when you return. Or, suppose you've had no thought of buying a bird and a sudden whim overtakes you in Paris while strolling along the Seine past the bird market. Within moments you are transformed from just another tourist into the proud owner of a magnificent bright-green parrot. Write this happy news to your vet immediately and ask him to mail back that statement. These precautions are suggested because it *is* possible that your pet will be detained until you can furnish proof that a licensed veterinarian will supervise or administer its treatment.

Now you're back on U.S. soil, and the quarantine officer agrees that your parrot is a fine, healthy-looking bird. But looks aren't everything with psittacines. You will have to certify that your pet will receive chlortetracycline or some other approved medicine for at least 45 days.

If you've had your pet for *at least 90 days immediately before arrival* you may have it treated in your home or at your vet's, as you prefer.

If you've had the bird for *less than 90 days before arrival,* you *must* leave it with your veterinarian for the duration of its treatment.

Needless to say—but they always do—the expenses for the treatment, in either situation, are all yours.

OTHER BIRDS

There are no regulations on nonpsittacine birds, just import duties, which you can include in your duty-free allowance.

Canaries valued at $5 or less will cost you 8 cents *import duty* each. Canaries valued at more than $5 will cost you 5% of their purchase price. Any other bird will cost 4½% of its purchase price. The rates quoted here went into effect as of January 1, 1972.

MONKEYS

These regulations cover monkeys, lemurs, baboons, chimpanzees and all other subhuman primates.

The quarantine officer will examine your monkey for signs of yellow fever or any other disease communicable to man. He will then ask where you've been to see if your monkey has traveled through a yellow-fever zone. If you have not visited a yellow-fever area, your pet will be admitted with no further ado. The latest list of yellow-fever-infected areas is as follows:

SOUTH AMERICA	AFRICA
Argentina	Cameroun
Bolivia	Ghana
Brazil	Liberia
Colombia	Mali
Peru	Nigeria
Surinam	Senegal
Venezuela	Togo
	Upper Volta

If you bought your monkey or were living or traveling in one of the countries listed above, your monkey must meet one of the following conditions:

(a) at least 9 days have elapsed since he left a yellow-fever zone, or

(b) he must arrive in a "mosquito-proof structure"* and

* The openings in a "mosquito-proof structure" are covered with 2 layers of sturdy wire screen, with not less than 18 wires per inch each way. The layers should be at least 1 inch apart. Or the openings may be covered with an outer layer of strong fine-mesh wire screen and an inner layer with sufficiently small openings so that the monkey can't extend any part of its body to within less than 1 inch of the outer layer.

have been confined to it for at least 9 days immediately before arriving in the States, or

(c) the monkey must have been effectively inoculated
against yellow fever.

If you are importing a monkey, the *import duty* is 3½% of
the purchase price as of January 1, 1972. You may figure this
into your duty-free allowance.

AMPHIBIANS, REPTILES AND PET RODENTS

The quarantine officer will simply examine such a pet to
see if it is free from communicable diseases and ticks, fleas or
other skin parasites.

WILD ANIMALS

"*Wild* refers to all creatures living in the wild state; or to
all creatures that, whether raised in captivity or not, are normally found in the wild state," as defined by the U.S. Bureau
of Sport Fisheries and Wildlife.

Animals that fit this definition are inspected by the quarantine officer at the port of entry to see if they're free from communicable disease. That's all—unless you're *importing* the
animal.

Importing Wild Animals

Before you are beguiled into buying a wild animal while
abroad, be sure to check the endangered-species list (see
pages 260-64) to see that your potential pet is not mentioned on it. If it is, and you've bought it, there's very little
chance at all that you'll be allowed to keep it. You'll have to
go through an extremely long and tedious process to prove it

would be an economic hardship for you to do without the animal. Pleading that you've always wanted a blue-nosed wallaby just isn't going to pass muster.

If you buy a "wild" animal that is not one of an "endangered species," be sure to keep your invoice or bill of purchase. Have copies made of it if you can.

In addition, you will need one (and we suggest you get copies for this, too) of the following documents from the country of origin:

(a) an export permit, or

(b) a document from an appropriate government official stating that the wildlife was lawfully taken, transported or sold, or

(c) a consular certificate from an American consul stating that the wildlife was lawfully taken, transported or sold.

Whichever document you obtain must be in English or you must have a certified English translation attached to the original.

Once your pet has been inspected by the quarantine officer, you'll be sent to the Customs Collector to fill out form 3-177, "Declaration for Importation of Fish and Wildlife." You then give the completed form plus copies of your invoice and entry document to the District Director of Customs right there at your port of entry.

As of January 1, 1972, the *import duty* on "wild" animals is 3½% of their purchase price. This may be applied toward your duty-free allowance.

INDEX

About the Authors

PAULA WEIDEGER has been doing research for this book ever since her first trip home from camp—with several salamanders. Her school days were filled with a parade of stray dogs who weren't allowed on the bus. Miss Weideger now lives in Manhattan with Cat, and Louie, a poodle.

GERALDINE THORSTEN teaches and lives in New York City with some stay-at-home tropical fish and her poodle traveling companions, Twiggy and Lorenzo.